The Lighthouse Movement

Multnomah® Publishers *Sisters, Oregon*

THE LIGHTHOUSE MOVEMENT
published by Multnomah Publishers, Inc.

International Standard Book Number: 1-57673-633-4

Cover images by PhotoDisc
Book design by Stephen Gardner

Scripture quotations are from:
The Holy Bible, New International Version (NIV)
©1973, 1984 by International Bible Society,
used by permission of Zondervan Publishing House
New American Standard Bible (NASB)
©1960, 1977 by the Lockman Foundation
The Holy Bible, New King James Version (NKJV)
©1984 by Thomas Nelson, Inc.
Holy Bible, New Living Translation (NLT)
©1996. Used by permission of Tyndale House Publishers, Inc.
All rights reserved.

Printed in the United States of America

For information:
MULTNOMAH PUBLISHERS, INC.
POST OFFICE BOX 1720
SISTERS, OREGON 97759

99 00 01 02 03 04 05 — 10 9 8 7 6 5 4 3 2 1

Foreword

A few days ago, I visited some of America's best known lighthouses in Maine. They're well kept, beautiful, majestic beacons of light. The staff members are anything but curators of museums. After all these years, they know they still have a vital mission. They're commissioned to help save lives. The same is true for you and me!

I applaud the vision behind the growing evangelistic Lighthouse Movement and urge you to read this book. Philippians 2 convinces me that the Lord wants Christians everywhere to:

- Humble ourselves as Jesus did;
- Lay aside our petty disagreements;
- Reclaim the truth of the gospel;
- Ask the Holy Spirit to fill us;
- Become blameless and pure;
- Live like children of God;
- Share the word of truth;
- Keep shining brightly!

The vision of this movement? To create at least 2 million lighthouses across America!

The mission? To pray for, care for, and share Jesus Christ with every man, woman, young person, and child in America by year-end 2000.

In this handbook, you'll be introduced to a variety of proven, practical evangelistic ideas that you and your family and your church can pursue in your neighborhood and community. What you'll read in this book isn't merely theory, believe me! Working hand in hand with thousands of churches and tens of thousands of individuals and families across America, evangelists such as Billy Graham, Franklin Graham, Greg Laurie, and myself have seen dozens of cities become ablaze with God's glory. Cities where the TV network affiliates report thousands of conversions to Jesus Christ. Where the daily newspapers present the life-changing gospel message clearly and compellingly. Where a God-consciousness permeates every level of society.

These fires are now spreading across whole states. A little over a year ago, a small group of Christians in Portland, Maine, invited us to help them light a fire in their city. We urged them to spread the vision to others. When all was said and done, some 10,000 Christians fired up for what newspapers described as the largest outreach in that state's history. It was, by many accounts, the greatest evangelistic event ever held in Maine, the Maine *Sunday Telegram* reported. As a result, more than 5,600 men, women, and youth across the state made a public commitment to Jesus Christ. In turn, they're sharing the light of the gospel with others. A once spiritual dark corner of America is shining brighter these days!

On the eve of a new millennium, it's more important than ever that we let our light shine across this whole land. I challenge you to read this book. Then, prayerfully commit yourself to becoming a lighthouse in your neighborhood, your community, your city, your state. And urge others to join you. The result will be a much brighter nation tomorrow!

Luis Palau
Luis Palau Evangelistic Association

Preface

A Call to Lighthouse Ministry

I've got something to tell you about that I believe will change the face of the Christian church forever. It's something new. Something radical. Something that will change how we approach reaching a lost world for Christ. It's something I believe God has put on my heart and the hearts of literally thousands of God's people in our nation.

I'm talking about lighthouses. I'm talking about neighborhood light centers—literally millions of them—that can be used to lovingly, compassionately, and appropriately point our neighbors to the saving, healing, forgiving power of Jesus Christ. I'm talking about neighborhood centers of prayer, fellowship, and evangelism where people of God meet the physical, emotional, and spiritual needs of their neighbors.

Nautical lighthouses are designed and built to be different from one another—different silhouettes, different intensity and colors of the light. That way, knowledgeable captains can recognize a particular lighthouse and determine their location. Likewise, your neighborhood lighthouse should also be different from others, simply because you live in a neighborhood that is in so may ways different from any other. It's *your* neighborhood, and it's filled with *your* neighbors, each of whom has his or her own set of problems, needs, desires, and perceptions of God.

A neighborhood lighthouse is nothing more than a household that takes spiritual responsibility for its neighbors by…

- Being neighborly, not isolated;
- Being accepting and encouraging, not judgmental;
- Being prayerful, not exclusive of anyone;
- Being focused on the Lord Jesus, not on denominational distinctives;
- Being founded on faith in Christ, not proselytizing or church recruiting;

- Being reconciled of offenses, not ignorant of God's way of dealing with offenses;
- Being a servant of neighbors, not ignorant of neighborhood needs.

As you read this, you may be thinking, *That sounds like a great idea! But how can I get involved? How can I make my home a lighthouse for my neighborhood?*

The answer to those questions isn't as complicated as you might think. It's simple, really. All we are saying is that you pray for, care about, and share the gospel with your neighbors—any way you see fit! And we're not only asking you to consider starting a lighthouse in your neighborhood, we're providing this book as a resource to help you figure out how God might be directing you to do it.

This book is a compilation of thirty-five writings by godly individuals we believe our Lord has given a special lighthouse vision. Each of these people has something to say about what it means to be a lighthouse keeper, what it means to take on this awesome responsibility of being a beam of light in your own corner of the world. Many of the writings give advice and instruction, and some of them provide phone numbers you can call, addresses you can write, and Web sites you can visit as you endeavor to become a lighthouse keeper.

If you feel a tinge of anxiety at the thought of embarking on this important ministry, you're not alone. Most people do! Becoming a lighthouse in your own neighborhood is an awesome, exciting calling, one that you shouldn't take lightly. But it's a calling I would encourage any follower of Jesus Christ to heed.

It's an exciting, enjoyable opportunity to get to know your neighbors better and to make sure that every one of them has a chance to hear the gospel. It's a way to obey Christ's command to us to tell people about him.

And the rewards for being a lighthouse in your neighborhood? Well, they're out of this world!

Dr. Cornell (Corkie) Haan
National Facilitator of Ministry Networks

One

Welcome to Lighthouse Keepers

—DR. PAUL CEDAR—

Do not gloat over me, my enemy! Though I have fallen, I will rise. Though I sit in darkness, the LORD will be my light.

MICAH 7:8

Welcome to the wonderful world of lighthouses!

I am delighted to introduce you to a significant movement, one we believe is initiated by our Lord. "Mission America" is a growing coalition of some 386 Christian leaders representing seventy-one denominations and more than 300 other Christian ministries and churches.

In addition, there are now some fifty-seven ministry networks involved in this unprecedented coalition. The focus of the Mission America movement is to encourage followers of Jesus Christ in the United States to allow God to use them by coming together to collaborate in the ministries of prayer, revival/spiritual awakening, and evangelism.

Our major initiative for the remainder of this century is called "Celebrate Jesus 2000." The vision we believe our Lord has given us is "to mobilize his church in America to pray for every man, woman, young person, and child by name—and then to lovingly and appropriately share the gospel with each of them by January 1, 2001."

Although there are many approaches and strategies being used to help fulfill this vision, through various denominations, ministry networks, cities/communities, and local churches across the nation, there is one strategy that has become the highest priority. It is the ministry of lighthouses.

That is what this manual is all about—LIGHTHOUSES!

We believe the ministry of lighthouses is a "God thing." Over the years, various ministries have used the term lighthouses to identify different types of outreach and evangelism. I was first introduced to the concept of neighborhood lighthouses twenty years ago by the dean of a theological seminary where I was teaching as an adjunct professor. He and his wife had become a part of a movement of Christians who established their homes as "lighthouses" for what they called "hospitality evangelism." They prayed for their neighbors for some time and then invited them to be guests in their homes. Within that context, they shared the gospel of Christ with them at an appropriate time. It reminded me of a ministry that my wife, Jeannie, and I had carried on for some time with neighborhood evangelistic Bible studies.

Then, a few years later, the Navigators produced a video curriculum called "Your Home a Lighthouse," which was a training course for evangelistic Bible studies. In more recent years, Ed Silvoso of Harvest Evangelism has introduced "Light Houses of Prayer." In addition, Al Vander Griend and John DeVries have given leadership to Mission 21 Hope, which focuses upon launching and servicing lighthouses. At the same time, Mary Lance Sisk, Evelyn Christenson, and other leaders of the AD 2000 Women's track have launched a lighthouse approach called "Love Your Neighbor."

As I write this chapter, some seventy denominations and ministries involved in Mission America have already established the goal of launching more than three million lighthouses during the next few months. This includes the Southern Baptist Convention, Promise Keepers, and Campus Crusade. Other denominations, Christian ministries, and churches are joining the movement daily. Only our Lord knows how many lighthouses will be established by the year 2000.

The concept of the lighthouses as related to Mission America is based upon the commandment of our Lord Jesus, who made the following statement in the heart of his well-known Sermon on the Mount:

> *You are the light of the world. A city on a hill cannot be hidden. Neither do people light a lamp and put it under a bowl. Instead they put it on its stand, and it gives light to everyone in the house. In the same way, let your light shine before men, that they may see your good deeds and praise your Father in heaven. (Matthew 5:14–16,* NIV*)*

When we were children, many of us sang this truth in a wonderful little song that said, "This little light of mine, I'm going to let it shine, let it shine, let it shine." Then the song continued to paraphrase the teaching of Jesus:

> *Hide it under a bushel? NO! I'm going to let it shine.*

In simple terms, that is what the lighthouses are all about. Our Lord Jesus Christ has commissioned us to let his light shine through us wherever we are—in our neighborhoods, schools, offices. The lighthouses are a wonderful vehicle to help us allow our light to shine more brightly and effectively.

This manual will introduce you to some practical ideas for launching and carrying on a lighthouse. You can be a significant part of what we believe is a God-initiated network of literally millions of lighthouses that are being established throughout America. At present, they are spreading across the nation like wildfire.

Although there are various expressions of lighthouses, most of them have at least three common denominators. They are:

1. Prayer. Christians involved in lighthouses pray regularly for some of their neighbors—or friends in their office—or classmates at school. They are encouraged to pray that the Lord bless their neighbors and friends and open their hearts to him.

2. Care. As Christians pray, they can look for opportunities to love their neighbors and friends by responding to their needs with the love and grace of Jesus. It is good to follow the example of Jesus who always met people at the point of need or interest—and to love authentically as Jesus did.

3. Share. Lighthouse Christians are encouraged to be alert for opportunities to tell others about what the Lord has done in their lives. Then, as led by the Holy Spirit, they can invite their neighbors and friends to join them for an outreach event or service in their church—or give them a *JESUS* video, a portion of Scripture, or a gospel booklet or Christian book that responds to their particular needs or interests.

Can you imagine what our Lord could do through a movement of millions of such lighthouses throughout America? As Ed Silvoso has said, such a movement of prayer could dramatically change the spiritual climate of this nation. It could also result in a great spiritual harvest. We pray that it may be so—for the glory of Jesus Christ and the advancement of his kingdom.

This is just a brief introduction to the wonderful world of lighthouses. Please read on to receive all kinds of practical ideas and suggestions for your lighthouse. And please pray with us that literally millions of lighthouses will be established throughout America in the next few months. Let us pray together that the Light of the World, Jesus Christ, will be lifted up so that literally millions of men, women, young people, and children will "see the light" and turn to him!

Welcome to the wonderful world of lighthouses!

Dr. Paul Cedar is chairman of Mission America and the author of several books, including the Mastering Ministry series and the Mastering the New Testament.

Two

Why Lighthouses?

—DAVID GIBSON—

Again Jesus said, "Peace be with you!
As the Father has sent me, I am sending you."

JOHN 20:21

Where will you spend eternity? What about your neighbors? How about your family? Unless our neighbors, friends, and family hear and respond to the Good News of the gospel, they face a frightening eternity without Jesus. And if we really believe what he says about salvation—"I am the way, the truth, and the life. No one comes to the Father except through Me" (John 14:6, NKJV), and "Salvation is found in no one else" (Acts 4:12, NIV)—what are we going to do about it?

The vision of Celebrate Jesus 2000 is "to mobilize the church to pray for and share Christ with every person in America by the end of 2000." What a God-sized task that is! It's a task that will take the commitment of millions of Christians to see it to completion.

I believe God is bringing the body of Christ together as never before, and Mission America is an example of that. Mission America is a growing coalition of over 350 national Christian leaders who represent seventy-two denominations (with some 180,000 local churches), more than 200 parachurch ministries, and fifty-six ministry networks.

These denominations and ministries are mobilizing individuals and local churches to establish three million lighthouses to reach 260 million Americans—every person in the nation—by praying for, caring for, and sharing the gospel with those in their immediate area.

Why three million lighthouses? We estimate that three million lighthouses will give full coverage of the United States if each neighborhood lighthouse were to reach five dwellings to the left, five to the right, and ten across the street.

The local church is key to this effort. Lighthouses provide an exciting way for local churches to launch their members into prayer and ministry opportunities in their own neighborhoods. As Christians become more active in their neighborhoods and communities, the local church becomes more visible and more relevant to those in need. We are asking the Lord to raise up 100,000 lighthouse churches. As pastors share this vision with their church, it's our prayer that each church will establish at least thirty lighthouses.

Thousands of lighthouses have already been established in communities across the country, and tremendous stories of the movement of God are being told. I believe that as God blesses this effort, the three million lighthouse goal could very well expand to become five to ten million lighthouses!

The lighthouse is not a new concept. It is a concept firmly rooted in Scripture. Jesus said to his followers in Matthew 5:14, "You are the light of the world. A city on a hill cannot be hidden." While the name may be slightly different, the concept of Christians reaching out into their neighborhood and community has been around since the first-century church.

The three basic elements of the lighthouse strategy are also from Scripture: to pray for our neighbors; to seek ways to show neighbors and friends that we care through acts of friendliness, kindness, and hospitality; and, as these friendships develop, look for open doors to share with them God's love and the gift of salvation he offers to them and how they can receive it.

We believe that the Lighthouse Movement is not so much a program but a movement of God's Spirit. The lighthouse must be made up of Spirit-controlled and empowered believers who have a vision to pray for, care for, and share Christ with their neighbors. The movement of God's Spirit through a revived church and individual believers reaching out in Christ's love through these lighthouses will result in spiritual awakening in our nation. I strongly believe God is raising up an army of believers with this burden and vision, which will reach potentially millions for Christ. I believe this is truly a "God thing."

Getting Started

A lighthouse is a gathering of one or more people in Jesus' name for the purpose of praying for, caring for, and sharing Jesus Christ with their neighbors and others in their sphere of influence. The primary focus of lighthouses is to establish a presence of Christ in every neighborhood. A lighthouse may also be established in a church, business, school group, or other setting.

Establishing a lighthouse is as easy as:

- **Praying**
- **Caring**
- **Sharing**

Begin by assessing who the people are in your neighborhood and other relational networks, such as workplace, school, etc. Write down their names and begin praying for them. You may want to try prayer-walking your neighborhood (walking around and praying for your neighbors and their homes) or prayer triplets (a consistent meeting to pray with two or three other Christians for the salvation of others). When appropriate, you may give neighbors the opportunity to share prayer requests with you.

Next, care for your neighbors through acts of kindness or hospitality, through serving their needs, or through the Canning Hunger program. Finally, seek to share Christ with them. As God opens the door, look for opportunities to share the gospel. Share your testimony and a simple gospel tract. Distribute the *Jesus* video. Invite them to church or an outreach event. In all things, seek to lovingly and appropriately share Christ with them.

Once you have decided to establish your home as a lighthouse, you will want to record your commitment with Mission America. We can keep helpful information and encouragement coming your way as you light the way. You may register your commitment electronically (www.lighthouse-movement.com), or write Mission America at 5666 Lincoln Drive, Suite 100, Edina MN 55436, or call 1-800-995-8572. Ask for the lighthouse commitment form. As soon as we receive the completed form back, you'll be officially registered. There is also a tear-out card at the end of this book that you may use to request the form.

When Jesus left this earth, he had one passion for his followers: that they shine out as beacons of light to the lost world he left behind. Just as Jesus is the Light of the World, every one of his followers is to be a point of reference—a lighthouse—showing the way home to him. That's what establishing a lighthouse is all about.

I believe that as the new millennium approaches, we find ourselves uniquely positioned for one of the most important efforts in the Church Age. You can play a key role in the most massive, intensive, and inclusive evangelistic outreach in the history of our nation. Don't let the opportunity slip by. Establish your home as a lighthouse today!

David Gibson is a team leader for Celebrate Jesus 2000/Mission America.

Three

Many Lighthouses Will Light Your City

—Reverend Glenn Barth—

You are the light of the world. A city on a hill cannot be hidden.

Matthew 5:14

The phone rang in my Minneapolis office one day in mid-June, 1998. It was Mark Godshall and Terry Inman of the Fremont/Tri Cities Association of Evangelicals (FTCAE). "Glenn," Terry said, "We're ready to take the next step forward in our city-reaching movement and we need your help. Could you bring leadership from the Mission America coalition to help us as we seek to launch a lighthouse in every neighborhood in our area?"

This call was an answer to the prayers of several hundred pastors involved with "Pray the Bay," pastors who had met with Dr. Paul Cedar in a prayer summit in January. As they prayed, they sensed God confirming a vision to strategically pray for and share Christ with every one of the 5.3 million people living in the nine counties of the San Francisco Bay Area.

It was an answer to the prayers of our Mission America team of national facilitators and of leaders in the Prayer Evangelism movement—people such as Ed Silvoso, Dave Thompson, and Dick Eastman. We sensed God calling us to hold the Mission America annual meeting in San Francisco. We felt the Lord had provided Pray the Bay as a model of how God uses a citywide movement to mobilize the church to pray for and lovingly and appropriately share the love of Jesus Christ with every person in their city. The vision for launching three million lighthouses across the nation needed a citywide model that leaders from around the nation could look at firsthand. We were praying for the Lord to open the door with an invitation from local leaders, and God did not disappoint us.

Our Lord answered our prayers, and a partnership of uncommon vision was birthed. Local vision cultivated in a fellowship of roughly forty-five pastors and Christian leaders in the Tri-Cities of Fremont, Union City, and Newark—twenty to twenty-five miles southeast of San Francisco—came together with the regional vision of Pray the Bay and the national vision of Mission America. At each level, not only was there a deeply shared vision, but also a commitment to values that grew out of servant hearts.

The leaders in the FTCAE requested that Mission America hold a city-reaching conference to assist them with their Lighthouse launch. They asked for Ed Silvoso and Harvest Evangelism to provide the model they would emulate and for Mission America to provide the broad umbrella so that evangelicals, charismatics, and mainline church leaders would all feel they could come to the table.

When the City Reaching Conference on Prayer Evangelism took place January 18–20, 1999, it felt like a slice of heaven on earth. Twenty-six speakers had come at their own expense to take part in this training. A spirit of prayer permeated the environment as intercessors who had prayed for months prior to the conference met in prayer throughout the three days. The Christian Broadcasting Network and World Changers Radio covered the event and told the story of this launch in their broadcasts. Each evening, pastors participated with Mission America leaders on 50,000-watt KFAX radio to guide couples and families in establishing their homes as lighthouses.

The conference served as a catalytic event in a steady-handed, prayer-based process that sees the establishment of 4,500 lighthouses, or one for every 100 people in the Tri-Cities, as a central strategy for reaching people with the love of Christ. Mark Godshall, President of FTCAE, recently told me that the conference helped the churches in their area more than double the number of lighthouses in their area from 600 to more than 1,400.

The vision for lighthouses is spreading across the nation, as seen in the following examples:

▸ Daniel Bernard, executive director of Somebody Cares in Tampa Bay, reports that more than 1,500 lighthouses have been registered in Tampa, Florida.

▸ Bishop George McKinney told me recently that his church is establishing more than 2,000 lighthouses in urban neighborhoods near St. Stephen's Church of God in Christ in San Diego. Prayerwalking efforts there have already resulted in a dramatic drop in violent crime to the extent that Police have come to Bishop McKinney to thank him and encourage his church in this effort.

▸ Jim Mulkey, executive director of Hope 2000 in Dallas has worked with pastors prayer groups seeking to launch 40,000 lighthouses. They have divided the Dallas/Fort Worth area into eight regions and are providing Lighthouse training through Houses of Prayer Everywhere in each one.

▸ In the Twin Cities of Minneapolis and St. Paul, Minnesota, "Celebrate Jesus Twin Cities," a coalition of more than 300 churches and ministries is in the process of establishing 26,000 lighthouses.

▸ The lighthouse flames are leaping across the prairie, as well, through The Prairie Lighthouse Project, led by Gayle and Larry Schuck in North Dakota.

As one who works with groups of Christian leaders in cities and communities across the nation, it has become clear to me that lighthouses are a strategy that God has given us for this time in history. America needs to be reevangelized. There is no better way to carry the message than prayerfully and lovingly going neighbor to neighbor. Pastors love lighthouses because they are a church-based and sustainable way for churches to grow through conversion. The testimonies of those who make their homes lighthouses inspires others to step out in faith to witness to neighbors through a prayer-care-share lifestyle.

Finally, when churches work together, the result will be belief (John 17:21–23). Christ-changed lives will lead to Christ-changed cities and ultimately to a nation permeated and changed forever by the love of our Lord and Savior, Jesus Christ.

The Reverend Glenn Barth is national facilitator of City/Community Ministries, Mission America.

Four

Lighthouses of Prayer

—Ed Silvoso—

My prayer is not for them alone. I pray also for those who will believe in me through their message...

John 17:20

As a young Christian, I knew I was supposed to witness to others. I also felt that I had been called to the work of evangelism. I even suspected that I had the gift of evangelism, but I could not picture myself witnessing door to door, as many Christian leaders around me had encouraged me to do. Even though I felt a desire that was at times a consuming passion for sharing the gospel with the lost, I could not see myself doing it cold turkey.

In my holy desperation, I was driven to the Scriptures, where I found instructive relief in the evangelistic model Jesus presented in Luke chapter 10. Let's take a look at Jesus' words in verse 2: "The harvest is plentiful, but the workers are few. Ask the Lord of the harvest, therefore, to send out workers into his harvest field" (NIV).

Please note that Jesus saw nothing wrong with the harvest. He described it as "plentiful," which is the highest compliment one can use to describe a harvest. My main fear was of rejection by those I was sent to witness to, but in this verse Jesus says that people are ready to hear the gospel. In another passage (John 4:35), he says that the fields are white unto harvest. Jesus is saying that people are ready to be harvested. So, where is the problem?

To find the answer, picture a farmer whose fields are pregnant with the most extraordinary harvest. It is harvesttime and something must be done to bring in the sheaves. Unfortunately, since he has no intention of going into the fields to gather the harvest, he has focused all his energy and resources on expanding the barns. He foolishly believes that the ripe stems will cut themselves loose from the ground and crawl on their own into the barns to be neatly stacked in rows. He sees his responsibility only as providing adequate barn space, and he holds the harvest responsible for finding it.

This example may seem nonsensical, since something like that would never happen on a real farm. Unfortunately, though, it is happening in the spiritual realm.

The church, if it is to reach the world for Christ, needs to agree with Jesus that there is a huge harvest waiting to be gathered. The greatest obstacle to seeing this harvest gathered is twofold: the church's inability to believe that there is a plentiful harvest out there waiting to be brought in, and its focus on building larger barns rather than deploying harvesters into the ripe fields. This causes harvesters (like I was) to be threatened by the unfounded fear of rejection and by a siege mentality that makes the barn more attractive than the ripe fields.

If there is no problem with the harvest, where is the problem? Some may say that it's the fact that the workers are few, since Jesus said so. However, *few* does not mean that their number is *inadequate,* at least to launch the harvesting process. By instructing his disciples to pray to the Lord of the harvest "to send laborers into His fields," Jesus identified the problem: The workers were not in the harvest fields. Since there were no workers to spare (they were few) all of them needed to be in the right place. The problem, then, lies with workers waiting for the harvest to come to them rather than the other way around—much like the farmer above.

The solution is to get the workers to go to the ripe fields, and the impetus to do so, comes from the first word in Luke 10:3. "GO!" Jesus said, "I am sending you like lambs among wolves." This constitutes a one-two punch: Pray to God, and go to the lost. God never intended for us to sit down and just pray. He expects us to pray while we go to the lost.

In the same way that lambs are extremely reluctant to approach wolves, Christians are reticent about spending time with the lost and, consequently, they never enter the very fields they are called to harvest. To make sure that this unhealthy attitude is reversed, Jesus' instructions in Luke 10:2–9 are very specific. He tells us to do four things:

- To bless the lost (v. 5)
- To fellowship extensively and unhurriedly with them (v. 7)
- To meet their felt needs (v. 9a)
- To proclaim the gospel (v. 9b)

Jesus said to begin not by witnessing to the lost, but by blessing them. This was to be followed by fellowshipping and meeting their felt needs, and only then by witnessing. What is our problem today? We have reversed the order of things. We begin with step four without going through the first three, and we get nowhere.

This four-step approach constitutes the backbone of prayer evangelism as implemented through lighthouses of prayer. Prayer evangelism is *talking to God about our neighbors before we talk to our neighbors about God*. This is best done by Christians turning their homes, workplaces, or campuses into a lighthouse of prayer. A lighthouse of prayer is a place where a believer, a couple, or a family have taken responsibility for the lost in their immediate circle of influence. This approach allows for the workers to move into the closest field to gather the harvest, where they spend the bulk of their time and where they have developed most of their relationships.

How feasible is it to reach your neighborhood for Christ through prayer evangelism? Any church that has staged a play like "Heaven's Gates, Hell's Flames" knows that multitudes are eager to receive Jesus. The harvest is plentiful. The challenge at hand is to move the workers to where the harvest is. Lighthouses of prayer allow Christians to do so.

At the turn of the last century, D.L. Moody and A.T. Pierson launched a process aimed at seeing America and the world reached for Christ before the new century. Sadly, by 1898 they had concluded that even though the resources were available to do it, they lacked adequate prayer. Today we stand on the same threshold. Let us not fail. Let us light the nation with lighthouses of prayer so that the task at hand will be carried out. The harvest is plentiful!

For more complete Lighthouse Training Material, contact Harvest Evangelism to request the *Light the Nation One House at a Time* Starter Kit (includes seven-minute video, thirty-minute audio, and instructional booklet).

Harvest Evangelism
P.O. Box 20310
San Jose, CA 95160-0310
1-800-835-7979
Fax: 408-927-9830 • E-mail: HarvEvan@aol.com
Or visit our Web site at www.HarvestEvan.org

Ed Silvoso is founder and president of Harvest Evangelism.

Five

Watching, Walking, Warring–and Winning

—Dick Eastman—

For though we live in the world, we do not wage war as the world does.

2 Corinthians 10:3

The tragedy of Columbine High School in Littleton, Colorado, in April 1999, underscores the need for the positioning of intercessors—lighthouses of prayer—throughout every neighborhood of every community across our land.

One wonders what might have happened if the two troubled youths who perpetrated the massacre had been consistent targets of specific, focused prayer from a nearby lighthouse of prayer. We know that both of these teens considered themselves outcasts, rejected by most classmates. Imagine the difference it might have made if believers in their neighborhoods as well as fellow classmates who knew Christ had targeted them with both prayer and periodic blessings on a consistent basis.

We know prayer can reach even the most troubled of teenagers—even those in the darkest of circumstances. Indeed, one of the slain teens at Columbine High, Cassie Bernall, only two years earlier had been deeply involved in a clique similar to the Trenchcoat Mafia, the group linked to the assailants involved in the Columbine massacre. The clique Cassie Bernall had joined was steeped in witchcraft, the occult, and a preoccupation with suicide. But Cassie became the target of prayer by desperate parents, friends, and a local youth pastor. To the amazement of the youth leader, Cassie showed up unexpectedly at the end of a church service and joyfully declared, "You'll never believe what just happened!" She then explained how she had surrendered her life to Christ.

As tragic as the loss of Cassie Bernall was, we see in this tragedy the power and influence of praying people on those blinded by demonic darkness. This demonstrates how lighthouses of prayer and outreach in every neighborhood of our nation could well be the key to dispelling this darkness by shining the bright light of Christ's healing and love.

One thing is clear as we look at the sometimes dark spiritual climate of our nation: Lighthouses of prayer and outreach are desperately needed, and they could be the key to America's next great awakening.

It all starts with prayer—and it's the kind of prayer that watches, walks, and goes to war.

The Watching Factor

The apostle Paul wrote, "Devote yourselves to prayer, being watchful" (Colossians 4:2, NIV). The word watch in this context suggests staying awake and standing guard. The Old Testament frequently described watchmen positioned on city walls keeping alert to potential enemy attacks (See Isaiah 62:6, 7). Jesus also stressed the need to both "watch and pray" (Matthew 26:41). Lighthouses make this possible in our neighborhoods.

The Walking Factor

Once we've determined to establish a lighthouse of prayer and outreach, we need to prayerfully move out into our neighborhoods. Prayer walking is an excellent way to begin. Prayer walking can be defined as simply walking through your neighborhood, praying for every house you walk past.

There is something about the "power of positioning" when it comes to spiritual and geographical issues. We recall God's promise to Abraham, "Go, walk through the length and breadth of the land, for I am giving it to you" (Genesis 13:17, NIV). And when Moses died, God said to Joshua of the Promised Land, "I will give you every place where you set your foot" (Joshua 1:3, NIV).

Prayer walking is indeed a vital aspect of establishing a lighthouse of prayer and outreach because it especially helps us to understand and apply the next important factor in "lighting our streets."

The Warring Factor

All prayer that ultimately confronts the darkness that keeps people from finding Christ involves some level of spiritual warfare (2 Corinthians 10:4, NIV). And we must never forget the ultimate focus for our "warring." It is the only thing that is truly eternal—the soul of a person.

Evelyn Christenson, in her guide *Evangelism Prayer*, not only provides a sound biblical case for praying for our neighbors, but suggests many of our evangelism efforts might be unfruitful because we do not properly employ two spiritual weapons. Those weapons are the authority of the name of Jesus (John 16:24) and the authority of the blood of Jesus (Ephesians 1:17, Revelation 12:11). I would add another weapon to the list: the authority of the Word of God (Ephesians 6:17, Revelation 12:11). This involves the tactical use of the Scriptures in our spiritual warfare, something that can be easily applied while prayer walking.

In all our warfare, we must keep in mind that we are warring to "loot the enemy's camp." Our hearts must be focused on the harvest. And that leads us to our final factor necessary to "light our streets" for Jesus: Winning!

The Winning Factor

Indeed, one primary purpose of Holy Spirit empowerment is to win the lost. Christ promised his disciples, "But you will receive power when the Holy Spirit comes on you; and you will be my witnesses in Jerusalem, and in all Judea and Samaria, and to the ends of the earth" (Acts 1:8, NIV). Here, witnessing for Christ is inseparably linked to the empowerment by the Holy Spirit. We later see the early church touching every household with the Good News (Acts 5:42).

One excellent tactical approach to begin prayer evangelism activities through your lighthouse is the Luke 10 model Ed Silvoso examines more fully in chapter 4 of this guide (see Luke 10:5–9).

Throughout this guide, there are a variety of ideas and models that will help you pray for and then reach and win your neighbors for Jesus. The point is to get started today by determining to establish a lighthouse of prayer and outreach right where you live, study, or work. Before long, you could well see your street (school, place of employment, etc.) aglow with the bright light of Christ's transforming love.

Dick Eastman is international president of Every Home for Christ and chairman of Light Your Street Project, Mission America.

Six

Lighthouses & Promise Keepers' Vision 2000

—BILL MCCARTNEY AND GORDON ENGLAND—

You are the light of the world.

MATTHEW 5:14

Promise Keepers strongly believes that Christians have a critical role to play in reversing the current moral and spiritual free fall in our nation. Today, our culture is in desperate need of the healing and restoration that only Christ can provide. The Bible and history tell us that significant cultural change can start with just one person who is sold out to almighty God. As we approach a new millennium, will you be that person? Jesus told His disciples "You are the light of the world" (Matthew 5:14). Do we take him seriously? How can we light the darkness together in such a way that the world will come to know Jesus? (John 12:32, 46)

We have seen God move powerfully in the past ten years, and His work among men has been an important component. Millions of men have attended Promise Keepers conferences across the nation since 1990, and tens of thousands have committed their lives to Jesus Christ. In a shifting moral landscape, men need to anchor themselves and their families to a bedrock commitment. That's why we're challenging men at the 1999 Promise Keepers conferences to "choose this day" to serve the Lord with all their hearts, no matter what. More important than any event is a life of promise keeping—for us to know what it means to be a man of integrity at home, at work, and in the world.

Promise Keepers calls men to commit to Seven Promises that summarize a man's relationship to God, family, other men, church, and community. Men tell us that one of their greatest needs is to grow in their commitment to Promise 7:

A promise keeper is committed to influence his world, being obedient to the Great Commandment (Mark 12:30–31) and the Great Commission (Matthew 28:19–20).

As part of fulfilling this commitment, we, in partnership with the hundreds of denominations and ministries of Mission America, are calling all Christian men and women to establish their homes as lighthouses. A physical lighthouse stands as a lasting beacon of light, security, and help. A Christian home is a spiritual lighthouse that shines the light of Jesus through prayer, caring, and sharing the gospel. Promise Keepers hopes to play a substantial role in establishing millions of lighthouses across America by the end of the year 2000.

In addition, we are preparing for Light the Night—a nationwide event on December 31, 1999. This event can be a rallying point for all lighthouses and we believe will result in the establishment of tens of thousands of additional lighthouses. It will also bring thousands of churches together in an unparalleled experience of unity and fellowship.

In 1997, PK envisioned churches gathering on capitol steps across the nation on January 1, 2000. Over time, this vision has been prayerfully refined into a celebration that could be much bigger and which could have more impact than we ever dreamed. We invite and challenge churches across America to band together in multichurch Light the Night gatherings on New Year's Eve, 1999. A gathering could be three churches or thirty churches. Whatever the size, the purpose of the gathering will be fivefold:

1. To express the unity of the body of Christ. Jesus prayed in John 17:23, "May they [believers] be brought to complete unity to let the world know that you sent me and have loved them even as you have loved me." Participating churches will create their gatherings in fellowship with other congregations of different cultures, ethnicities, and denominational traditions.

2. To celebrate the presence of God among his people. The gatherings will focus upon exultant praise, worship, and prayer. Having a hope like no other, we plan for a celebration like no other.

3. To look back with thanksgiving and look forward with faith. We have much to thank Him for. Facing challenging times, we must join hearts and hands to serve Him together, come what may.

4. To listen for God's message for our times. Pastors and congregations will prepare for the gathering by praying for God to inspire a timely proclamation of His Word. To this end, Promise Keepers is also preparing a special Light the Night video, that will feature a special message by leaders from a broad spectrum of the body of Christ.

5. To prepare for a powerful expression of ministry on January 1, 2000. On this first day of the year, we hope to see all Christian lighthouses begin it by consecrating themselves to the Lord, then by praying for the needs of their neighbors. Imagine if every man, woman, young person, and child in America would be the object of prayer and blessing on that day! After prayer, participating lighthouses will greet and bless their neighbors, showing care and support for each other, and inviting them to church where appropriate.

If the people of God respond to this challenge, the spiritual climate of America could visibly change in a day and churches would be overflowing on Sunday, January 2.

We are looking to the Lord for an era of spiritual revival. We believe the church should begin to prepare for it now. As Christian men and women commit themselves to the Lighthouse Movement and as churches prepare to Light the Night with multi church gatherings on New Year's Eve, we sense a growing momentum toward what could be one of the most significant spiritual seasons in the history of the church. Choose this day to let your light shine boldly!

For more information about Promise Keepers, visit our Web site at www.promisekeepers.org, or call 800-888-7595. PK has 15 men's conferences scheduled for 1999 from June through October.

Bill McCartney is founder and president of Promise Keepers. Gordon England is executive director of Lighthouses.

Seven

Lighthouse Partnerships

—DR. CORNELL HAAN—

A cord of three strands is not quickly broken.

ECCLESIASTES 4:12

It's important to know that you are not alone! You are not the only lighthouse in the world, or your city, or your neighborhood. The United States Post Office has identified 28,500 five-digit residential zip codes. With about 30,000 lighthouse churches each asking their members to be a lighthouse in their neighborhood, there should be three to six million lighthouses like yours.

See! You are hardly alone!

Realizing that you are not alone, it is also important to realize the strategic importance of working together. Don't be the Lone Ranger lighthouse. There seems to be a special anointing on people who humbly follow Jesus serving together. The natural man with a strong ego finds the facilitative leadership style of partnering unnatural. So here are some hints to help you in learning to work effectively with other lighthouses:

- Give place to another's gifts. That eliminates the need for competition.
- Remove the need to look good, but desire for Jesus to look good.

- Value uniqueness, not conformity and uniformity.
- Replace your controlling personality with brokenness and repentance.
- Be mutually accountable to each other.
- Maintain relationships best with a climate of prayer.
- Expect variety in ethnic and cultural values.
- Be flexible and less concerned about your position.
- Lead by listening and helping others accomplish their goals.
- Ask questions instead of giving answers.
- Take responsibility rather than authority.
- Give yourself and your ministry away to anyone who will take it.

Your lighthouse is invited to become a partner on four levels. First, you are invited to partner with a variety of major national ministries, many who are mentioned in this book. Choose those that fit you and your neighborhood. Contact them. You are now a partner with them.

Second, you are invited to partner with the churches and the other lighthouses in your city. Unfortunately, it is likely that some neighborhoods will have several who volunteer to be lighthouses, while others will have no one. If the pastors in your community are functioning in unison, they will have this information. They will need your help in establishing a lighthouse in every neighborhood. Call your pastor and discuss the problem. Then, volunteer like a short-term missionary to establish a lighthouse in an unreached area. If the pastors are not functioning in unison, you could be the catalyst to mobilize the Christian leaders in your community. Hundreds of cities now have a person called of God serving full or part-time to mobilize that city as a city pastor. There are about 4,000 cities and communities in our nation with a population of 15,000 or more. National leaders communicate with about 1,500 pastor's prayer groups that gather each week to pray for their city. No doubt there are more! Lighthouse keeper, you are now a partner with the pastors in your city.

Third, you are invited to partner with the other Christians and lighthouses in your neighborhood. If one of your Christian neighbors is not an official lighthouse, ask them to send in one of the cards in the back of this book. The strongest lighthouses can be in neighborhoods where one or more lighthouses meet to form an outreach strategy. Warning! It is possible to enjoy meeting together with your Christian neighbors so much that the others be ignored or treated as second-class friends.

After you establish which homes are likely Christian—notice I did not say "good" or "bad" or "Lutheran" or "Baptist" homes—plan a strategy meeting. Here's a sample agenda: 1) get acquainted, 2) pass out a database prayer list of your neighbors, 3) pray for them by name, and 4) discuss by asking, "What would please God, if we..." and "What can we do better together than on our own?" For example, things like a block party, Y2K preparation party, Christmas party, and Promise Keeper's New Year's Day Prayer Time is best done together.

Fourth, you are invited to be a partner with the Lord himself. Think ahead. It's the year 2005. You were some of the first to establish a neighborhood lighthouse in your city. Now some friends planned a reunion for the entire lighthouse family that have come from that original group. Hundreds attended. Unrealistic? Not really. Some of the original group moved and established a new lighthouse. Others invited friends from across town. They discovered Jesus and established their lighthouses also. But where is the real reunion? In heaven!

You are not alone! Stay in touch with national ministries providing resources, your city pastor, and other lighthouse keepers. But most of all, stay in touch with God!

Dr. Cornell Haan is compiler of this book and the national facilitator of Ministry Networks for Mission America/Celebrate Jesus 2000.

Eight
Lighthouse Adventure

—DAVID R. MAINS—

I have become all things to all men so that by all possible means I might save some.

1 CORINTHIANS 9:22

I remember the first time I understood the exponential power of the lighthouse concept. Several pastors from the greater San Francisco area were explaining how the Lighthouse Movement called "Pray the Bay" had captured not only them but also the people of their congregations. "This is truly a God thing!" one of them said.

I was attending the 1999 Mission America annual meeting. I recall thinking as I sat there, *I believe the Lord could well have given a simple tool to his church that literally sparks revival in the land.*

About six months earlier, we had chosen to make evangelism the thrust of our 50-Day Spiritual Adventure for the year 2000. We had taken Mission America's theme of "Celebrate Jesus" and used our eight Adventure Sundays to answer the question, "What made Jesus so attractive?"

The sermon topics unfold this way:

1. He stayed spiritually connected and directed. Jesus was in tune with the Father, praying and obeying. In the same way, we need to keep in touch with the Lord, getting our marching orders from him.

2. He shattered the stereotypes of "us" and "them." Jesus boldly stepped across the social boundaries of his day, connecting with Samaritans, women, Gentiles, and "sinners." We have different categories today—racial, social, denominational, political—but we should be just as courageous in crossing them.

3. He liked people and drew out the best in them. Jesus was a people-builder. Instead of criticizing who people were, he saw what they could become. We ought to be as winsome as he was.

4. He knew his identity, yet served with humility. Jesus was the divine Son of God, but he stooped to wash his disciples' feet. We are privileged to be called God's children, but we must not put on airs. Let's follow our Master into servanthood.

5. He spoke God's truth in everyday language. Jesus used words people could understand. Too often Christians develop their own "religious" lingo. As we offer the good news of Jesus, we need to make sure people get it.

6. He cast a vision of a better kingdom, now and in the future. Jesus taught about the kingdom of God, where grace would flourish and people would commit themselves totally to a new way of life. We invite people today to be part of that kingdom, to find peace and fulfillment under Jesus' rule.

7. He courageously completed his assigned mission. Jesus stepped steadily toward the cross in brave submission to his Father. God gives us various jobs, and they're not always easy. We must draw on his strength to perform them.

8. He broke the power of darkness so all can live in the light. Jesus fought the forces of evil and won a brilliant victory. He burst from the grave, robbing death of its sting! In a world blinded by pride, greed, and lust, we can invite others to live in the light of Christ.

Following the Mission America California conference and now understanding a little of the power of what lighthouses of prayer could do, I recommended that we make the action steps (or application aspect of these adventure sermons) revolve around helping participants establish and maintain Lighthouses of Prayer. I was amazed how easily the concept fit with our already established preaching themes and journaling assignments.

Think what it would be like to have everyone in your congregation be challenged through both the preaching and individual journal-keeping to establish a Lighthouse in their neighborhood just like you already have. To obtain information about the 50-Day Spiritual Adventure program and how it has positively influenced tens of thousands of congregations, call 1-800-2CHAPEL. Ask specifically about the one called *Celebrate Jesus—the most attractive person ever.*

David R. Mains is executive director of the Chapel Ministries, a nonprofit organization that equips churches through various media ministries.

Nine

Who Is My Neighbor?

—CHRIS COOPER—

The King will reply, "I tell you the truth, whatever you did for one of the least of these brothers of mine, you did for me."

MATTHEW 25:40

Anyone who does not know Jesus personally is headed for a Christless eternity. They are like the man Jesus told us about who was beaten and left to die on the road. Fortunately, a Samaritan cared enough to stop and help save his life (Luke 10:25–37). We are to be like that Samaritan.

Jesus told us to "love our neighbors as ourselves." That love is to be shown in our telling people about the message of salvation through Jesus. But who are our neighbors? Surely, all people are our neighbors. They desperately need the Good News of Jesus Christ, and it is our responsibility and privilege to carry that good news to them.

Intentional Acts of Love

We all have opportunities to build relationships with our neighbors if we intentionally make a reason to meet with them. The concept of the lighthouses is that Christians would pick out the equivalent of twenty households around their own home for whom they will pray, provide care, and share the gospel by the end of 2000.

But how to keep track of those households? Neighborhood prayer lists are available through the Mapping Center for Evangelism and Church Growth. Based on your address, you can receive a list of your "prayer walk-able neighborhood," including a specific list of your closest twenty-four households. You'll also receive a demographic analysis of your neighbor-hood to give you insight into the prayer needs of your community.

This list will contain the names and phone numbers for the households that are listed in the White Pages. The households with nonpublished phone numbers will have an address only. As you meet the people in those houses you can update your list. When you request your list, you will be registered as a lighthouse. A donation of $10 is suggested when you ask for your neighborhood prayer list.

An advantage of registering as a lighthouse is you will then be able to discover other lighthouses in your area. Here is a story of how Christian households worked together to reach their neighbors.

A Shared Vision

In the spring of 1996, we had the idea of gift wrapping a *JESUS* video, putting it with a plate of cookies, and delivering it to our neighbors in Kansas City with a personal note during the Christmas season. My wife and I invited three other Christian neighbor households to our home for dessert. We showed them a short clip of the *JESUS* video and asked them if they would be willing to take four houses around them. The idea was to pray for those homes, work on our relationships, deliver the video at Christmas, and then look for an opportunity to follow up.

The first family said, "Ever since we moved into this neighborhood, we've wanted to have some form of outreach. We just never felt equipped and so we never got started." The second family said the same thing. The third family said, "We already give cookies to seven homes, so we would be happy to add a *JESUS* video. But we know some other Christian homes in our neighborhood. Why don't we ask them if they would like to participate?"

We left that meeting with a list of eleven Christian homes from nine different churches. After our third meeting, we had seventeen Christian homes that distributed more than seventy *JESUS* videos at Christmas. That scenario was multiplied throughout the Kansas City area. Thousands of Christian homes from several hundred churches participated in the distribution of more than 40,000 *JESUS* videos (as well as more than a quarter of a million cookies).

A result of the process we used, which was as important as distributing the *JESUS* video, was that all of these Christian families were encouraged to discover each other. And the Lord gave us a common vision of our neighborhoods as mission fields.

That is a vision we hope is shared by Christians around the country.

Reaching Every Home

In order to accomplish the goals of Celebrate Jesus 2000, Christians in our nation's neighborhoods need to meet each other and make sure that all of the other homes are covered with prayer and the light of the gospel. We at the Mapping Center for Evangelism and Church Growth want to help make that a reality by offering helpful resources.

The Mapping Center can provide your church or ministry with a Kingdom Combine CD-ROM that is custom built for your extended harvest field. Please call to request a kit of information. To order your Neighborhood Prayer List, check with your local Christian bookstore or Christian radio station, or visit the Mapping Center's Web site at mappingcenter.org. Also, you can call 888-627-7997.

Another resource you may want to consider is the video by Pastor Ted Haggard on "The Power of Prayer Walking."

Chris Cooper is president of the Mapping Center for Evangelism and Church Growth, based in Lenexa, Kansas.

Ten

Lighthouse Communications Network

—Naomi Frizzell—

Also in Judah the hand of God was on the people to give them unity of mind to carry out what the king and his officials had ordered, following the word of the Lord.

2 Chronicles 30:12

Communication is a key part of the Lighthouse Movement. As a coalition of ministries and denominations, we want to make sure you have access to resources that will help you effectively pray and share your faith. And, we want to share encouraging stories with you about how God is working in and through lighthouses. Remember, as you commit your home to be a lighthouse, you are the key to the communications process of lighthouses in your neighborhood.

Don't be a solo lighthouse! Join with your Christian brothers and sisters by following these four simple steps:

1. Register your lighthouse at www.lighthousemovement.com. Registering your lighthouse helps us track involvement in your community and allows us to serve you better by providing resources you need to reach your neighborhood. While this Web site is in its preliminary stages, it's our prayer that this site will become a central place for communication to and from your lighthouse and a resource for prayer and evangelism tools.

2. Use Mission America's monthly newsletter, The Lighthouse. This newsletter will keep you up to date about the Lighthouse Movement, point you to effective resources and share exciting stories of how God is using lighthouses just like yours. (For a free subscription to *The Lighthouse,* write to: Mission America, 5666 Lincoln Drive, Suite 100, Edina, MN 55436.)

3. Send us stories of how God is using your lighthouse so we can share the stories with other lighthouses. (E-mail me at: nfrizzell@compuserve.com, or mail to: Mission America, 5666 Lincoln Drive, Suite 100, Edina, MN 55436.)

4. Encourage other Christians you know to become a lighthouse by sharing this booklet with them, encouraging them to visit the Lighthouse Movement Web site, or by calling Mission America at 800-995-8572.

Hundreds of Mission America coalition members are using their communication channels to share the message with their members. While the examples of such involvement are too numerous to mention, the following gives you a good idea of how God is drawing his body together:

- World Changer's Radio (the radio voice of Campus Crusade) has now become the Voice of the Lighthouses. Dr. Bill Bright and Dr. Steve Douglass are doing a wonderful job sharing the lighthouse vision and giving practical suggestions for being an effective lighthouse. (Check your local Christian radio station to see if they carry the program.)
- Pray magazine (The Navigators) is committed to lighthouses and is producing a special lighthouse issue in the fall of 1999. (Call 800-691-7729 for subscription information.)
- The *JESUS* video project has developed a lighthouse *JESUS* video packet. (Call 888-JESUS-36 for more information.)
- Chapel Ministries is dedicating its annual 50-Day Spiritual Adventure to lighthouses in 2000. Call 1-800-2CHAPEL for more information.

Promise Keepers, The Southern Baptist Convention, Evangelical Covenant Church, The Joseph Project, and many, many others are fully in support of this exciting God-sized effort and are a part of the Lighthouse

Communications Network.

Mission America wants to help you brighten the light in your neighborhood. Stay informed and stay involved through the Lighthouse Communications Network. We're here to serve you, we're here to connect you with others, and we're here to encourage you.

Naomi Frizzell is national facilitator of communications ministries for Mission America.

Eleven

Starting & Sustaining a Lighthouse

—DR. ALVIN J. VANDER GRIEND—

They devoted themselves to the apostle's teaching and to the fellowship, to the breaking of bread and to prayer.

ACTS 2:42

If you've decided to start a lighthouse of prayer, I applaud you. You're starting something that will bless your neighbors, grow your spiritual life, and glorify God. I know it will make a difference. Prayer always does!

A pastor in Walnut Creek, California, decided to start a lighthouse by taking five minutes a day to pray five blessings on five neighboring households. After eight weeks of praying he reported that one person had asked him how to have a personal relationship with Jesus Christ. He led her to Christ. Another person asked for his help to get out of drug dealing. A Buddhist couple from across the street asked to go to church with him, and a searching couple next door asked him to start a Bible study for neighbors.

You may not have such dramatic and immediate results as that when you start your lighthouse of prayer, but you can be sure that things will happen when you pray that wouldn't have if you hadn't. That's God's promise, and it is the way he has chosen to work.

What is a lighthouse? It is a cluster of two or more believers, banded together to pray for, care about, and share the blessings of Christ with their neighbors.

Here are nine steps to start and sustain your lighthouse:

1. Make a commitment. Tell God that you are committed to making your home a lighthouse by praying a prayer like this:

"God, I know that my neighbors matter very much to you and that you have commanded me to make 'requests, prayers, intercession, and thanksgiving' for them. So, out of obedience to you and out of love for my neighbors, I commit myself to ask for your blessings for my neighbors. I'll do this, with your help, to the best of my ability. In Jesus' name, amen!"

God will certainly honor such a prayer.

2. Begin simply. Try the five-'n'-five prayer challenge: praying five blessings for five neighbors, five minutes a day, five days a week, for five weeks. Think of the word bless to remember five important ways to pray for your neighbors:

Body—health, protection, strength
Labor—work, income, security
Emotional—joy, peace, hope
Social—love, marriage, family, friends
Spiritual—salvation, faith, grace

3. Mark your house. Identify your home as a lighthouse by putting the lighthouse decal or the lighthouse model in your window. These will send a message that your neighborhood is being prayed for.

4. Establish your "prayer" neighborhood. Write down the names and addresses of those you will pray for. Do some research. Find out what is going on in the neighborhood. Create a simple map of your "prayer" neighborhood.

5. Connect with your neighbors. Personally connect with neighbors by simply asking them for prayer requests. Most people today are pleased to be asked. Prayer walking your neighborhood—walking around praying for homes and people you see—will get you out to pray "on sight within sight." Doorhangers* or prayer greeting cards* will inform your neighbors that you are praying for them.

6. Record prayer requests and answers. Record specific prayer requests and answers in the Pocket Prayer Journal* or keep your own personal journal. Share your prayer answers with others.

7. Pray, care, and share. Make yourself available to God, and he will lead you into ministries of caring and sharing as well as praying. You'll have a threefold impact. By praying, you'll release God's grace into people's lives. By caring, you'll build bridges of love to them. By sharing the gospel, you'll help people come to know Jesus Christ.

8. Expand the numbers. Maximize your potential by expanding the number of people you are praying for. Be aware, however, that there is a limit. You can handle only so many felt-need requests and neighbor relationships. Expand also the numbers you are praying with. Find other Christians who are ready to join in prayer.

9. Strengthen your prayer life. The stronger your prayer life, the more impact you will have in your neighborhood. Always pray with a clean heart, with compassion, and with persistence. The book *Developing a Prayer-Care-Share Lifestyle** is designed specifically for this purpose.

Please join the ranks of believers who are starting lighthouses of prayer. Make a difference! Let your light shine right where God has placed you!

**Items are available from Homes of Prayer Everywhere (HOPE). Phone 1-800-217-5200, Fax: 616-791-9926. You can contact our Web site at www.hopeministries.org.*

Dr. Alvin J. Vander Griend is director of HOPE Ministries and author of several books.

Twelve

Reach 3—An Engaging Offer of Christ

—Patrick Morley with Geoff Gorsuch—

But I, when I am lifted up from the earth, will draw all men to myself.

John 12:32

Before you read any further, would you do me a favor? I know that as a lighthouse leader, you have been praying for people in your neighborhood. But I'd like you to identify the names of three colleagues in your "professional neighborhood" you also care about. Please write their names on the lines provided here.

1. ______________________________

2. ______________________________

3. ______________________________

We'll come back to them and talk about how you can influence them for Christ. But first, let me tell you a story:

In the fall of 1995, I sensed a strong desire to see if the leaders of the Christian men's movement would like to meet. After much prayer, I called

Dr. Glenn Wagner, then the vice president of Promise Keepers, and he agreed to be involved in future discussions. I began to call other men's ministry leaders.

Over the years, I have learned that any time someone thinks they have a unique message from God . . . they don't. Whenever God speaks, he puts his message into the hearts and minds of thousands of his children. So it was encouraging to discover that every man I called had also been thinking we should talk.

Finally, in January of 1996, we met for the first time, in Atlanta. Toward the end of that day Dr. John Tolson said, "What would excite me is to explore the question, 'What can we do together that none of us could do alone?' " The room lit up like Times Square on New Year's Eve!

Since we all agreed that our real passion was to reach men for Jesus Christ, the question became, "How can we reach every man in America with the gospel?" The answer, of course, is that we can't. But God can! And, with that in mind, a group of us later began the Orlando Coalition of Men's Ministries. Our guiding question was "How can we reach every man in Orlando with the gospel?" After much prayer, a new strategy was born.

Reach 3!

We all agreed that we needed an idea that was simple enough to make men say, "I can do this," but big enough for them to say, "Wow! How can I be part of that?" We needed a vision and strategy that was simple, intentional, focused, concrete, and motivational, but one that reflected God's calling. It also needed to be inexpensive to implement, inclusive of the church, and easy to use. It seemed impossible!

We began to develop and field-test a simple relational evangelistic strategy very similar to the "prayer, care, and share" model currently used in neighborhood lighthouses. Using this model, large numbers of Christian men began reaching their peers for Christ. We called it "Reach 3."

Surveys revealed that there were twenty million adult Christian males in the country. Those same surveys indicated that that there were sixty million "unchurched" men in America. Therefore, if every believing man reached out to three of his peers, in a short time it would be possible to credibly present the gospel to every American man. Using our field test as an example, we saw that it could be done.

How does it work? It's as simple as it sounds. In fact, the entire strategy fits on the front and back of a wallet-sized card.

Seven Steps to the Reach 3 Strategy

1. Prayerfully identify three men you work with who you don't know are Christians.

2. Pray for their salvation every day.

3. Invite each to a "nonagenda" meal, just to get better acquainted.

4. When appropriate, ask each man for prayer requests. Check back with him.

5. Later, invite these men to outreach events, Bible studies, or church.

6. Continue praying and seeking opportunities to expose them to the gospel.

7. When they come to Christ, help them become more involved in church and discipleship opportunities.

Seeing the simplicity of this strategy, many of us in the Orlando Coalition of Men's Ministries exclaimed, "Hey, I can do this!" We started praying for and meeting with men all over the city.

The results have been deeply encouraging.

Will You Accept the Challenge?

Now, back to the three names you jotted down earlier. Would you be willing to prayerfully work toward the salvation of these three men? If yes, use a wallet-sized card (or a replica of the seven steps above), copy the three names to the card, and begin to follow the steps.

Will you bring the Reach 3 challenge to the attention of your church's leadership or the leadership of other neighborhood lighthouses? You can receive all the wallet-sized cards you need free of charge by calling us at 407-331-0095, ext. 15.

Please consider working with others, as we did in Orlando, to make a community-wide effort to bring this challenge to as many men as possible in your city.

Seeking Feedback

We're trying to record stories and testimonies of how God uses the Reach 3 challenge. Please write and let us know how it's going...and how we may be of help. As you contact us, here are a few questions to consider:

1. How did you meet this man?
2. What did you say to set the appointment? How did he respond?
3. What time of the day did you get together?
4. How did the meeting go? Any surprises?
5. How do you feel about this method for reaching men?
6. Where do you think your praying and this appointment will lead?
7. Permission to use this story (without real name): ____ yes ____ no

Be assured of our prayers for you and your ministry to the people in your neighborhood and to your colleagues at work. If there is anything we can do for you, don't hesitate to contact us at:

Man in the Mirror
154 Wilshire Blvd.
Casselberry, FL 32707

or

The National Coalition of Men's Ministries
Box 620398
Littleton, CO 80162

Patrick Morley is chairman and CEO of Man in the Mirror, a ministry for men. Geoff Gorsuch is executive director of men's ministries at The Navigators.

Thirteen

Lighthouses & Other Religions

—Dr. Joseph Tkach—

Simon Peter answered, "You are the Christ, the Son of the living God."

Matthew 16:16

In considering how we can best reach the hearts of people of other religions, we must remember that we are first and foremost lighthouses of prayer. As Dietrich Bonhoeffer explained in *Life Together*, our relationships with others cannot be other than selfish when they are direct relationships. It is only as we relate to others through Jesus Christ that we can have truly positive relationships—relationships of love—with them. That is why our primary task when reaching others with the gospel is to pray for them.

Unfortunately, some Christians tend to see their role in witnessing to people of other religions as more of a *confrontation* than a love relationship. It is as though they believe they are in some kind of spiritual kickboxing arena in which their faithfulness to God will be measured by whether they "defeat" this enemy. So they proceed to fire verses about the supremacy of Jesus in a verbal duel designed to back their "opponent" into a logical corner.

With this mindset, of course, the Bible becomes a mere tool we use to try to "win" an argument rather than the instrument of God's grace that he inspired it to be. And, of course, although we might feel gratified about having "declared" the truth to the infidel, any spiritual fruit borne of the encounter is in spite of our misguided efforts, not because of them. There is an old adage I think applies here, and it goes: "A man convinced against his will is of the same opinion still."

"Evangelism is you," Madeleine L'Engle once said. Being who Jesus made us to be is the most natural and effective way of showing others what faith in him is all about. It is when we let the Holy Spirit bear the fruit of God's love in us that we are truly witnesses of his miraculous redeeming work in the world.

In witnessing to people of other religions, here are ten key principles to keep in mind:

1. Jesus is not intimidated by other religions. We don't have to be, either. When we feel intimidated, we get defensive, and our approach becomes self-centered rather than Christ-centered. Christ in us can look past all the unsound beliefs and simply love.

2. Jesus loves the people who are in other religions. We can love them, too. When we are more focused on theological arguments and logical formulas than on the person Jesus loves, we lose Christ's perspective, and our approach becomes wooden and confrontational rather than genuine and caring.

3. The gospel is the message of the love and grace of God. A person who does not love the one to whom he or she is conveying the gospel cannot effectively convey it. Such love comes only from God.

4. The most effective evangelistic tool is prayer.

5. The best advertisement for the gospel is Christ in you. It's not some artificial performance for the sake of looking good—but the real you, including your problems and weaknesses, ministering in Christ's love to the real needs of others.

6. Attacking a person's religion or their religious leaders turns them off to you and to the message you bring. In many cases, the person's religion has brought a measure of order, peace, and blessing to an otherwise chaotic life. Most religions do contain, after all, important elements of morality and self-restraint that are not inconsistent with biblical principles. Respect that fact. It is a vital point of connection for eventually moving on to what all morality based religions lack: grace.

7. Your goal is to love the person in the name of Jesus, not to win a religious debate.

8. God prepares the heart and convicts the soul; our job is to minister God's love.

9. Remember the apostle Paul's admonition about how to talk with unbelievers. "Let your conversation be always full of grace, seasoned with salt, so that you may know how to answer everyone" (Colossians 4:6).

10. Live in such a way that a person might have cause to ask about the hope that lies within you.

As we become lighthouses, first and foremost, of humble prayer to our heavenly Father in the name of Jesus Christ, we can trust the Holy Spirit to fill us with the love, the grace, the wisdom, and the patience we need to minister the gospel effectively to people of other religions.

The Mission America Alternate Religions Track Web site (www.apologia.org/resources) gives helpful online, as well as offline (books, tapes, and pamphlets) resources for ministering to people involved in alternative religions.

Recommended resource: *Evangelism Through the Local Church* (Michael Green, Nashville: Nelson, 1992), especially chapter 3, "Evangelism in a Multi-Faith Society?"

Dr. Joseph Tkach is president and pastor general of the Worldwide Church of God. He is also author of the book Transformed by Truth *(Multnomah).*

Fourteen

Caring Lighthouses

—NORMAN WHAN—

I have compassion on these people.... I do not want to send them away hungry, or they may collapse along the way.

MATTHEW 15:32

God's Word says in Acts 1:8. "You will receive power when the Holy Spirit comes on you; and you will be my witnesses in Jerusalem, and in all Judea and Samaria, and to the ends of the earth.." God tells us in this verse to spread the gospel to the world by starting at home (our "Jerusalem") and moving outward (our "Judea" and "Samaria").

The Canning Hunger ministry was born out of my heart for evangelism and a desire to provide Christians with unlimited opportunities to be witnesses and to share Jesus Christ with their neighbors.

Dr. Paul Cedar, Chairman of Mission America: "Canning Hunger is being used by God to help Christians move from 'prayer walking to neighbors talking.' It enables each of us to 'turn our neighborhood into our Jerusalem.' "

Canning Hunger is a simple, non threatening, food collection strategy that helps you meet the needs of the hungry while meeting your neighbors under the best of conditions. By eliminating the fear of knocking on your neighbor's door, Canning Hunger is unleashing unprecedented potential for personal witnessing and evangelism.

As a lighthouse keeper, you select a number of homes in your neighborhood, dedicate yourself to praying for each home by address and every person by name, then share the gospel with each of them by year-end 2000.

I believe the greatest challenge in accomplishing our goals is "going from prayer walking to neighbors talking." It's my observation that mass evangelism programs struggle most when we have to go from our neighbor's sidewalk to their threshold. We all know how hard it is to knock on a neighbor's door and deliver a tract, invite them to church, or share our testimony. But what could be easier than asking them to help feed hungry kids and their families? Everyone wants to help with that!

The Canning Hunger Strategy

The Canning Hunger strategy is designed for lighthouse keepers to develop their route at their own pace. The strategy is simple: collect food to fight hunger and develop relationships that eventually earn you the right to effectively share the gospel.

Dr. Bill Bright, president/founder of Campus Crusade for Christ: "While prayer and fasting remain the foundation of spiritual revival, we inevitably come to a point where we must boldly and lovingly share the gospel message. The Canning Hunger strategy paves an incredible path for the messenger."

One successful approach starts with prayer walking, recording the addresses of each home on a form in our Lighthouse Keepers Kit, followed by seven personal contacts. The statistics show that this is an effective way to make the inroads you need to deliver the gospel message to your neighbors.

On your first visit, you introduce yourself to your neighbors using the script we provide and ask them to help in the fight against hunger with a food donation. More than 95 percent of the people who open the door give food on your first visit, and better than 99 percent of those who give initially invite you back on a regular basis.

The second visit you collect food. On your third visit, collect food and, using another script, ask your neighbor for prayer requests. Over 85 percent of them trust and respect you enough to share a prayer request the first time you ask.

The fourth and fifth visits are for collection of food and follow-up on prayer requests. On the sixth visit, using another script, report on the amount of food collected to date and give your neighbor a gospel gift of appreciation, such as the *JESUS* video. Better than 92 percent gladly accept your gift.

On the seventh visit, collect food, follow up on prayer requests, look for opportunities to present your testimony, and watch to see what God does with the seed you planted as you continue to "serve your Jerusalem."

Ending Hunger in America

The recent "National Research Study on Hunger," conducted by Harvest National, reveals that 32 million people suffer from hunger in America. The report indicates that the suffering could be eliminated with an additional 80 million pounds of food per month.

Our goal is to recruit, train, and equip at least 800,000 of the 3 million or more lighthouse keepers to develop a regular neighborhood food route of 20 to 30 homes. Six years of data, from thousands of volunteers, indicate a route of 25 homes averages at least 100 pounds of food per month. Eight-hundred thousand routes would produce the 80 million pounds of monthly food needed to end hunger in America. Order your kit today and be part of that solution!

The Lighthouse Keeper's Kit is free, and it includes reproducible masters containing scripts, tracking forms, name badge, "Yes, We Can" button, thank-you notes, reminder notes, hunger statistics, food distribution tips, and more.

To order, contact: Canning Hunger, 131 E. Grove Ave., Orange, CA 92865. Phone: 714-279-6570. Our fax number is 714-279-6575. You can E-mail me at norm_whan@canninghunger.org or visit our Web site at www.canninghunger.org.

Norman Whan is founder of Canning Hunger, a ministry that promotes evangelism through food collection for those in need.

Fifteen

Lighthouses for Women

—Evelyn Christenson—

Brethren, my heart's desire and my prayer to God for them is for their salvation.

Romans 10:1 (NASB)

The AD 2000 North American Women/Christian Women United network is made up of women from all denominations, organizations, and ethnic backgrounds, all working together to help reach every man, women, and child in the United States for Christ through prayer, acts of kindness, and verbal sharing of Jesus—in order to win the lost to him.

We believe the only hope for curbing the escalating violence and moral and spiritual darkness in our country is to have lives transformed by Jesus, who came to planet Earth as the Light of the World, saying, "I have come into the world as a light, so that no one who believes in Me should stay in darkness" (John 12:46).

Being a Lighthouse

When Jesus ascended to heaven, he already had said to his followers, "You are the light of the world" (Matthew 5:14). Jesus was saying it then, and he's saying it now: we are to be lights for him, and our homes are to be the lighthouses.

But how can our homes be lighthouses in our neighborhoods? Ordinary bricks and boards do not make lighthouses. They are the Light, Jesus, shining in believers from the house and into the neighborhood, city, and the rest of the world (Acts 1:8, Colossians 1:27).

Christian Women United realizes the need to reach a lost world for Jesus. But how can one woman—or even a small group of women—help? How can we be lighthouses for Christ?

God is powerfully using our simple yet profound "Triplet" and "Love Your Neighbor" methods around the world to reach people for Jesus Christ:

▸**METHOD 1: Triplet prayer.** This is from my book, *A Study Guide for Evangelism Praying* (Harvest House). This is a very powerful method of praying for the lost, and it involves a trio of devoted believers praying together for unbelievers to come to know Christ. Three Christians each choose three unsaved people and commit to getting together at least fifteen minutes a week to pray for the salvation of their nine. Having partners who live, work, play, study, or worship together assures easy accessibility and accountability with no financial expenditure or elaborate organization.

For years, evangelism triplets have had great success. For example, in Mission England I in 1984, where 90,000 ordinary Christians prayed in triplets for one year before Billy Graham and Luis Palau's six crusades, both evangelists reported the greatest results ever to that time. Billy Graham's *Decision* magazine reported that many triplets saw all their nine accept Jesus before the evangelists even got there.

▸**METHOD 2: Prayer walking from your lighthouse.** This is taught in the Mary Lance Sisk book *Love Your Neighbor as Yourself,* and it demonstrates how one woman can impact her neighborhood by fulfilling the royal law of "You shall love your neighbor as yourself" (James 2:8). Radiating Jesus' light and love through prayer walking your neighborhood and deeds of kindness to your neighbor or friends is an unbeatable combination for reaching the lost with Jesus' salvation.

The Curriculum

Our national and regional training conferences have been equipping and mobilizing women for successful evangelism on every continent for over five years with the following simple, inexpensive two-part curriculum:

▸**Book 1: *A Study Guide for Evangelism Praying*** is helpful in that it biblically addresses:

1. Why we should tell others of Jesus. Jesus died to pay for the sins of the whole world, but left the telling everyone to us, his followers (Acts 1:8). Regardless of religious belief, all are condemned already until they come to Jesus for salvation (John 3:18), and that they will spend eternity in the lake of fire if they don't know him (Revelation 20:15). Accepting Jesus' forgiveness for their sins transfers them from Satan's kingdom of darkness to Jesus' kingdom of light (Colossians 1:12–14), with abundant life now and life after death in heaven (John 3:16).

2. The lifestyle God requires for results in praying and witnessing (1 John 3:22–23). It's vital to keep the grime off your lighthouse lenses! In order to have Jesus' light shine through you and your home, you have to know him personally, and knowing him, you live a life that is pleasing to him. The life you live will determine if your prayers for the lost are effective (James 5:16).

3. Dependence on the Holy Spirit. The Christian's power and the lost person's conviction of sin comes only from the Holy Spirit, not from our plans and programs (1 Thessalonians 1:5). We access the Spirit's power through prayer.

4. Pre-evangelism praying. God will hinder Satan's attempts to steal the gospel seed (Luke 8:11–12) and will remove the blinders that keep the lost from seeing the light of Christ from our lighthouse (2 Corinthians 4:3–4).

5. Praying for one another. This is essential, since evangelism is rescuing captives from Satan's kingdom (Ephesians 6:18–20).

6. Reproducing lighthouses. The study concludes by explaining how to biblically lead people to Jesus, disciple them, and make them soul winners. In other words, it tells us not only how to lead people to Christ, but how to make others into lighthouses for him.

▸**Book 2:** ***Love Your Neighbor as Yourself,*** by Mary Lance Sisk, puts feet to the biblical mandates of the study guide, mobilizing women to "love our neighbors as ourselves" by:

▸ Seeing your neighborhood as God sees it and realizing that your being there is no accident.

▸ Evaluating your neighborhood with a directory, and through mapping and communicating.

▸ Interceding for your neighbors personally and through prayer walking.

▸ Gathering others to pray in triplets, in neighborhood prayer groups, and at your churches.

▸ Having compassion for your neighbors, reaching them with living acts of kindness.

▸ Rebuilding relationships before sharing the gospel.

▸ Opening your heart and home through simple hospitality or Bible studies.

▸ Rejoicing with God when any neighbor accepts Christ.

Please join us and be a lighthouse for Jesus where you live! For more information or to order our books, contact us at:

Phone: 704-541-1023, Fax: 703-543-8077
Write: Love Your Neighbor, P.O. Box 472247, Charlotte, NC 28247-2247
E-mail: Msisk91242@aol.com

Evelyn Christenson is chairwoman of Mission America's North America Women's Track, founder and president of United Prayer Ministry, and author of **What Happens When Women Pray.**

Sixteen

Celebrating Children

—Dr. Virginia Patterson—

At that time Jesus said, "I praise you, Father, Lord of heaven and earth, because you have hidden these things from the wise and learned, and revealed them to little children."

Matthew 11:25

Yes, children are a light for Jesus! And they can also have lighthouses!

The vision of Celebrate Jesus 2000—to pray for and share the gospel lovingly and appropriately with every person in our nation by year-end 2000—cannot be achieved without making children a priority. Children under age fifteen make up one-quarter of the U.S. population.

An even more compelling reason to make children a priority is that Jesus places high value on them. Two incidents clearly demonstrate this.

To show his disciples who was the greatest, Jesus "took a little child and had him stand among them. Taking him in his arms, he said to them, 'Whoever welcomes one of these little children in my name welcomes me'"(Mark 9:36–37). Shortly after this example, it was necessary for Jesus to speak even more strongly to his disciples.

People were bringing little children to Jesus to have him touch them, but the disciples rebuked them. When Jesus saw this, he was indignant. He said to them,

"Let the little children come to me, and do not hinder them, for the kingdom of God belongs to such as these. I tell you the truth, anyone who will not receive the kingdom of God like a little child will never enter it." And he took the children in his arms, put his hands on them and blessed them. (Mark 10:13–16)

Jesus places high value on children, and we must follow his example. But as we endeavor to lovingly and appropriately share Christ with children, what biblical principles should we follow?

As a Mission America initiative, Celebrate the Child has defined some important principles and lighthouse applications to follow in ministry with children.

▸**PRINCIPLE 1: Any viable ministry with children must involve their family.** Families are the key vehicles for shaping children, and effective ministries with children must support and empower the family structure. In this setting it is easy to follow the model of Deuteronomy 6:7: "Impress them [God's commands] on your children. Talk about them when you sit at home and when you walk along the road, when you lie down and when you get up."

Lighthouse Application: Encourage entire families to establish Lighthouses of Prayer. Within the family, have children praying for children and youth praying for youth. That way, when the family gets to know other families in the community, children will naturally relate to the other children.

If there are other families in your community who are establishing lighthouses of prayer, you might join together with other lighthouse families. Then there would be opportunities for children to pray with children for other children in their neighborhood.

▸ **PRINCIPLE 2: The gifts of children must be celebrated and expressed.** God has given each child certain gifts and abilities that need exercise to develop. Families need to provide ways for their children to contribute according to their gifts and abilities to the family, and in turn to the other families in their neighborhood.

Lighthouse Application: In all of the activities and events you plan as a family—to pray for those in your community, to give gifts, to plan events, and to invite them into your home—identify how the gifts and abilities of your own children will be celebrated and expressed.

As you plan ways to get together with other families in your neighborhood, think of ways their children can be involved to express their gifts.

▸**PRINCIPLE 3: Children must be integrated into a nurturing community of believers.** The task of ministry with children goes beyond evangelism. Making disciples among children is the broad, long-term task of ministry with children. We cannot assume they will survive as individual believers. The community of Christ must accept them as full members and provide the supportive influences that will continue their discipleship growth.

Lighthouse Application: Most people—children and adults alike—attend church or church activities because a friend or relative invites them. After praying for and getting acquainted with the families in your community, invite them to your home or invite them to some church functions with you.

Families may attend church functions, such as special music or holiday programs, church picnics, or sports leagues. Children may be interested in summer day camps, vacation Bible school, or club programs. Parents might be interested in parenting study/support groups, aerobics classes, or single moms' groups. If children and their families attend some of the above activities, the next step is to invite them to church and Sunday school. As they begin to attend regularly, parents should be invited to join a small group. In this more intimate, informal setting, they get to know other adults, and begin to feel that they belong to the community of believers.

And we trust God that somewhere in this process, as Christ is lovingly and appropriately shared with them, they will receive Christ into their lives as Savior and Lord.

Not only do children make up a significant part of the church today, they are the church of tomorrow, as well as tomorrow's lighthouses. We dare not overlook them!

Dr. Virginia Patterson is president emerita, Pioneer Clubs.

Seventeen

A Lighthouse Christmas Party

—Norm Wretlind—

She will give birth to a son, and you are to give him the name Jesus, because he will save his people from their sins.

Matthew 1:21

"What in the world do we have to do to feel good about our relationship with our neighbors? Why don't you just take some initiative to witness for once?"

I was taking out my frustration on my wife, Becky. I had just returned from a very successful sales trip in which I had also boldly shared Christ with one of my salesmen. I had felt on top of it spiritually all week...that is, until I drove back into our neighborhood. Growing feelings of being a dishonest, "silent" Christian neighbor hung over me like a suffocating smog. We had lived on Lambda Lane for three years but had never once mentioned the name of Jesus to our neighbors. We had prayed for them and befriended them, but that wasn't enough. We were active in our church and could openly share our faith everywhere, but we froze up around our friends and neighbors. Why?

Soon our conversation became a heated argument. Accusations flew both directions. We both felt hopeless. She resisted my pushiness and I resented her cautiousness. Finally, after I got my emotions under control, we decided to pray and ask God for wisdom. Becky and I loved God and each other, and we really cared for our neighbors. We just did not know *how to* share Christ with them.

Not more than ten days later, a friend called to invite us to a Campus Crusade Lay Institute for Evangelism. It was an offer we couldn't refuse! We sensed God was up to something. Ultimately, that conference broke the log-jam. We learned afresh how to walk and witness in the Spirit. Most of all, we heard about how to share Christ in the context of a nonthreatening neighborhood party.

A party, Lord? Why, of course! Why didn't we think of that? That's a truly "neighborly way" of sharing Christ on our block. We decided right then to try it out at Christmastime.

December came. We passed out the invitations, and, to our surprise, almost everyone came! Some helped us decorate. People brought their favorite holiday foods. It did not feel like *our* party for *them,* but like a neighborly event held in our home. And since we were the hosts, we set the environment by stating in the invitations "beverages will be provided." Amazingly, not one person even mentioned alcohol. We were having too much fun playing icebreaker games and singing Christmas carols.

When everyone was feeling relaxed and nostalgic, I invited them to take turns talking about their favorite Christmas memories and traditions, or to talk about what Christmas meant to them. I included this topic so that I or other believers present could easily share our faith in Christ. The sharing time was very delightful and revealing. I concluded by telling my neighbors for the first time how Jesus Christ had become the center of my life and family. I was scared, but determined. Then I gave each a gospel booklet as a gift to take home.

Neither Becky nor I were prepared for what happened next. Seconds after I finished sharing, Marlis exclaimed, "I just became a born-again Christian two months ago! Now Christmas has a whole new meaning for me!" We had no idea of this, and neither did her husband. Within minutes other neighbors began talking about their interest in spiritual things. Before we knew it, a women's Bible study was planned to begin after the holidays.

Six months later, we were transferred to Dallas, but not before three neighbors placed their faith in Jesus Christ through that Bible study. Even more amazing, the woman who purchased our home accepted Christ through the influence of those ladies within the first two months she lived in the neighborhood. The following year she tracked us down just to thank us for starting that Bible study. When we set up our new home in Dallas we purposed in our hearts not to wait three years to begin sharing Christ with our new neighbors. We asked all our friends to earnestly pray that we would be a lighthouse for our neighborhood from day one. What happened over the next thirty-six months is legendary. It was like living in the book of Acts.

We initiated nine neighborhood parties over various seasons. Some were for adults and some were just for kids. That opened up many opportunities for one-on-one caring and witnessing. As a result, more than sixty neighbors from an eight-block area accepted Christ. Whole families came to faith, with each family influencing other families to believe. Lives were changed, marriages were saved, and children became loved and nurtured in the Lord. We all grew together through three neighborhood Bible studies. Incredibly, we counted forty-nine neighbors attending our church. Then came the day I will never forget. Dennis, our first neighbor to receive Christ, said during one of our couple's Bible studies, "Hey, why don't WE become a church?"

On a beautiful Sunday in September of 1976, more than 125 people attended the very first service of the new Richland Bible Fellowship church in Richardson, Texas. Most everyone walked to church. It was held at the neighborhood elementary school. We grew in numbers each week as believing neighbors continued to befriend and share with those around them. Soon we outgrew the school and bought the neighborhood tennis and swim club. Today, those tennis courts are parking lots, the pool is regularly used for baptisms, and the new facilities minister to more than 1,100 adults and kids every week.

Becky and I have discovered from these events that instead of feeling guilt and frustration about evangelism in our neighborhood, we could actually have fun witnessing to our neighbors. In fact, we learned that neighborly evangelism can be a party!

Norm Wretlind is president and founder of Neighborly Evangelism Ministries.

Eighteen

Lighthouses & Church Growth

—Dr. Larry Lewis—

And the Lord added to their number daily those who were being saved.

Acts 2:47

There are basically two ways to effectively evangelize a community. Likewise, there are two ways for a church to grow.

The first, and most traditional, is through "expansion." This is increasing the number of people who attend at the church building in the hope they will be evangelized through preaching, teaching, and worship. The second way—less traditional but far more fruitful—is through "extension." This is taking the church to the people rather than getting the people to come to the church. This involves the church breaking out of its fortress mentality and establishing preaching, teaching, and worship points throughout the community.

The concept of growing a church through extension rather than expansion is effectively embodied in the lighthouse strategy. Members are encouraged to make their homes "houses of prayer." Thus the church's mission and ministry are focused on the members' loving and caring outreach to their own neighborhoods. Members begin by praying for their neighbors by name, getting to know their neighbors personally, ministering to their neighbor's needs, sponsoring "get acquainted" events for their neighborhood, and—as the Lord leads—sharing a gospel witness. In so doing, the church's ministry is projected throughout the community.

The First Baptist Church of Arlington, Texas, now has more than 200 extension points throughout the Dallas/Fort Worth metro area. Although the mother church averages more than 1,000 in attendance, an additional 3,000 are touched through their many satellite congregations, some of which meet in the homes of the church members.

The legendary Charles Haddon Spurgeon pastored the great Metropolitan Tabernacle in London, England, during the last part of the nineteenth century and in the early twentieth century. In addition to pastoring the largest church in the world, he led and trained the members of his congregation in establishing more than 1,200 "preaching points" throughout London and southern England. Although many of these were started in member's homes, hundreds of the preaching points eventually became church-type missions and many became constituted churches.

Dr. Paul Chou is pastor of the largest and fastest growing church in the world. His congregation, the Yoido Full Gospel Church in Seoul, South Korea, averages more than 600,000 in weekly attendance and has a membership of nearly 1,000,000. How did they become the largest church in the history of Christendom? Supported by fervent and effectual prayer, they have filled Seoul with "house churches," (i.e., lighthouses) with literally thousands of their members opening their homes weekly for prayer, Bible study, and worship. At last count, there were more than twelve thousand lighthouses hosted and led by the members of this one church.

Of course, neighbors reached through lighthouse ministries will be encouraged to attend and unite with a local church congregation. As part of their discipleship ministry, the lighthouse keeper will make sure all new converts are congregationalized as well as evangelized. Thus, the church growth by extension will often enhance its expansion as new members are added to the church.

Who can know how many lighthouses may someday become churches?

God is in the business of growing large trees from tiny seeds. It certainly would not be surprising if neighbors gathering together for prayer and worship in somebody's home would not soon sense the need for a Bible preaching/teaching church in their community. Perhaps most new church plants have resulted from just such home fellowships.

Also, it would not be surprising if God were to use the Lighthouse Movement to birth thousands of new church plants across America. The need for hundreds of new churches is critical. In fact, to have the same number of churches in ratio to population today as we did in 1970, we need an additional 96,000 churches.

Establishing lighthouses of prayer, ministry, and outreach may well be the best strategy in place today to win this nation to Christ and minister to its needs. More effectively than any other, it is enabling the church in America to reach the Celebrate Jesus goal to pray for and sensitively share Christ with every man, woman, and child in America by year-end 2000.

Dr. Larry Lewis is national facilitator of Celebrate Jesus 2000/Mission America.

Nineteen

Fasting & Prayer in Your Lighthouse

—DR. BILL BRIGHT—

While they were worshiping the Lord and fasting, the Holy Spirit said, "Set apart for me Barnabas and Saul for the work to which I have called them."

ACTS 13:2

I believe the Lighthouse Movement could be one of the most powerful ideas the Lord has ever given his people, as powerful, perhaps, as the first-century church or as the closed country house churches of today.

May I humbly suggest a weapon that can make your lighthouse especially powerful—as powerful as a spiritual atomic bomb?

I am referring to the explosive power of fasting with prayer. The Lord has given us the discipline of fasting with prayer to destroy the strongholds of evil and usher in a great revival and spiritual harvest around the world. When approached with the proper motive, the discipline of fasting and prayer will supercharge your lighthouse.

In my life, I have seen the spiritual and physical benefits of fasting, as I have done at least one forty-day water and juice fast in each of the past six years.

I believe the lighthouses are a vital, God-given strategy to help fulfill the Great Commission. I relate Jesus' forty-day fast to the Great Commission. You will remember that Jesus did not begin his ministry until he had finished his forty-day fast. In the Great Commission, he commands his followers to teach what he taught, and that would, of course, include his forty-day fast. He is our mentor and model. If we want to pattern our lives after his life, fasting and prayer will be a very important priority for us. Further, fasting was very important both to God's people during the Old Testament era and in the first-century church. The leaders of the Reformation—Martin Luther, John Calvin, and, later, John Wesley—placed a strong emphasis on fasting with prayer.

I don't believe that any other spiritual discipline so completely meets the conditions of 2 Chronicles 7:14, "If my people, who are called by my name, will humble themselves and pray and seek my face and turn from their wicked ways, then will I hear from heaven, forgive their sins, and heal their land."

To help you, I offer seven important steps in any fasting and prayer effort:

1. Set your objective. As a lighthouse, let the spiritual objective for your fast support your lighthouse objective. Write it down and refer to it frequently.

2. Make a commitment. Ask the Lord what type of fast you should do. Should it be no solid food? Restricted solid food? Water only? Juice and water? Also, how long and how often should you fast. One meal a day? One day a week? For forty days? Ask him what other activities should you restrict, such as television and reading materials that do not contribute to your spiritual health. Also ask how much time each day will you devote to prayer and the study of God's Word. Make a commitment!

3. Prepare yourself spiritually. Humility and repentance are the keys to fasting and prayer. The Scripture commands us to humble ourselves (1 Peter 5:6). Ask the Lord to show you any unconfessed sins. Write them down. Confess them. Ask the forgiveness of others you may have offended, making restitution if necessary. By faith on the basis of God's command (Ephesians 5:18) and God's promise (1 John 5:14, 15), be filled with the Holy Spirit. Begin your fasting with an expectant heart.

Expect spiritual opposition from Satan, but appropriate the Lord's victory over him. Remember, greater is he who is in us than he who is against us.

4. Prepare yourself physically. Precaution is in order. Consult a physician if you are in poor health, especially if you are on medication or have a chronic ailment such as diabetes, lupus, or any number of ailments that could create problems during a fast. Several days before you begin your fast, begin gradually eating smaller portions. Especially avoid high-fat and sugary foods. Some advise eating raw fruits and vegetables for two days before beginning.

5. Put yourself on a schedule. Plan your different praise, worship, prayer, and Bible-reading times for morning, afternoon, and evening. Set times for each. Avoid distractions. Include times for nourishment, such as natural nonsugar juices and plenty of water.

6. End your fast gradually. Do not stop your fast all at once, as that can be traumatic to your body. Begin eating very gradually with soups and raw fruits and vegetables.

7. Expect results. Faith and expectancy are the seedbeds of prayer answers and miracles. As you have prayed according to God's will, expect—and look for—answers. By faith, thank him for the results.

I pray that our dear Lord will bless and guide you in your efforts to minister in your neighborhoods, and as you fast and pray, may your lighthouse be a powerhouse, to his great honor, glory, and praise.

Dr. Bill Bright is founder and president of Campus Crusade for Christ International.

Twenty

One View from a Lighthouse

—LLOYD OLSON—

The fruit of the righteous is a tree of life, and he who wins souls is wise.

PROVERBS 11:30

Well, it's finally Saturday morning—a beautiful day! I guess there's no way of putting it off. We have prayed about it. Now is the hour. I feel strange. Frankly, I feel outright fear.

Okay, get a grip. All Robin and I are going to do is walk out our front door, turn left, and up the block. We're giving JESUS videos to our neighbors.

We were serious when we decided to be a lighthouse in our neighborhood. The "prayer" part was fairly easy. I've been talking to God for years. And I guess we didn't do too badly in the "care" department. Robin has always maintained friendships with our neighbors. On the weekends I had often helped guys on our street with fix-it projects. But, the "share" part…that's a little threatening.

Two Hours Later

I never really wanted to meet Fred up the street. Even though I had never talked to him, I didn't like him. But, it's good to know that he coaches youth basketball. Maybe he and I could take our kids to a college game together.

I think Sally across the street really meant it when she said they look forward to watching the video. Wouldn't it be great if they responded like the family I read about? The mother said, "Jesus has changed our whole family. We can't thank you enough for giving us the JESUS video. The school office even called asking what had happened to make our daughter's attitude and grades improve so dramatically."

As we visited each neighbor's door, it sure was nice not to be put on the spot. I guess I may have let my imagination run away beforehand. No one asked any deep theological questions. No one got mad at us. Nobody laughed in our faces. In fact, most people seemed to genuinely appreciate our video gift. And why not? They rent videos all the time.

Now I know that each of our neighbors has access to a clear presentation of the Good News. And since the video is a dramatic motion picture, I know it's something they can enjoy and understand.

I wonder who on our street will be watching it this week? Will it be like the family of five I heard about? They crawled into bed one night to watch the *JESUS* video they had been given. Even though the father attended church regularly, he had resisted making a commitment to Christ. But that night, the video made it clear who Jesus is. At the end of the tape the entire family prayed the prayer and accepted Jesus.

Wow! Just reading the jacket of the video gets me excited! "Witness the most remarkable story of passion, intrigue, pain and glory as you are taken back two thousand years to the life of Jesus Christ . . . a masterpiece that was created by the Cannes Film Festival award-winning producer John Heyman and a team of specialists. Researched for five years and filmed in over 200 locations in the Holy Lands, this film soars you into an experience you will never forget."

Sort of like what happened to the crusty old guy I heard about. I think his name was Rudy. Seventy-one years old. The town handyman. He got a copy of *JESUS*. When he saw it he wept. Then he prayed the prayer to receive Christ at the end of the video. Several weeks later, Rudy was dead. Now he's with Jesus. I hope all of our neighbors will end up with Jesus.

Well, what now? I guess it's more prayer, care, and share. We should pray as a family that each of our neighbors watches the video. And I'll try not to be too anxious to ask our neighbors for a while, "Have you seen the video yet?" And, "What did you think of it?"

But, you know we never had considered our neighborhood as a group. And, it does seem right that our neighborhood should be a group with whom we are involved. When Jesus said we are to share the Good News of his love and forgiveness, he said we should start with our Jerusalem.

Tuesday Evening at the Small Group Meeting

Robin couldn't keep from talking about the people to whom we gave *JESUS* videos. Sam and Jane Edwards, who host our small group, said they would really like to start on their block. They invited us to come over next Saturday to prayer walk with them. Edna, a widow in our group, wasn't sure she could get going by herself. So, two of us couples agreed to help her out. I think of the eight couples and singles in our Bible study, there will be five or six lighthouses in a few weeks. You know, if the Bible studies, care groups, and some of the other folks at church get going, our church could have more than a hundred lighthouses.

I began to see what our pastor was saying when he told us that he thought the lighthouse strategy was a God thing. He said that the book of Acts said the early church not only went to the synagogues, but door to door. It just seems that being a lighthouse is something we should have always been doing.

Wednesday at the Office

"You know this lighthouse thing is really catching on," Ted said to me. Ted is a Christian friend of mine who attends another church in town.

"Yeah! I know," I said. I told him our experience last weekend. Then I said, "I've been wondering whether we could have a lighthouse right here in our office. We eat lunch together every day. I wonder if we could start praying for those that work in each of our offices."

As we talked it became more clear that this lighthouse thing could work in many of our relationships—our neighborhood, our office, the kids' coaches, team members' parents, those in our service clubs, our bowling team.

We got back early from lunch to look at the jesusvideo.org Web site to get more lighthouse ideas. And there we also heard about the 1-888-JESUS-36 number we can call to order more videos and have questions answered.

You know, I once heard that something like a 1,000-watt light bulb is all it takes to create the powerful beam of a lighthouse. Lenses and mirrors magnify the bulb to 50,000-candle power-a beacon that can be seen for fifteen miles.

That's what I'm praying for. I'm just going to turn on my light and ask God to provide the lenses and mirrors so others would see Christ.

Lloyd Olson is executive director of JESUS Video Project.

Twenty-One

Adopt a School for Christ

—PAUL FLEISCHMANN—

From the lips of children and infants you have ordained praise because of your enemies, to silence the foe and the avenger.

PSALM 8:2

Jesus' heart beats with compassion for our lost world. While he lived on earth, one of his main concerns was for the lack of workers, because the harvest was so plentiful (Matthew 9:36–38).

Today, the harvest is even more plentiful! Christian pollster George Barna reports that six out of ten teenagers want to be close to God and that 75 percent of those who receive Christ do so by age seventeen. Yet, tragically, only one-third of teenagers is involved in a Christian youth group (*Generation Next,* 1995). In other words, despite this obvious openness and thirstiness, most people are still headed for a Christ-less eternity, because they are not coming to our churches to seek out the gospel.

Evangelism is like a combine. For too many decades, we have kept that combine in the barn. From time to time, workers have gone out in the fields and have pulled up a few stalks of grain. They have returned to the barn to hand feed those stalks into the powerful combine.

If this is the way we continue to do evangelism, we will lose the majority of this generation. We *must* throw open the doors of our barns and get our combines into the fields. And, if we really want a big harvest, we will minister to youth. Statistics show that if people are not reached by the time they are teenagers, they are likely to never respond to the gospel.

While there are many ways to reach teenagers, it seems logical to go where they are—the school campuses—in order to reach most of them. That is the conclusion of the Challenge 2000 Alliance, a coalition of more than sixty denominations and youth ministries that are committed to communicate the gospel of Christ to every teenager. Specifically, they are asking God to raise up a ministry of evangelism and discipleship to every middle school, junior high, and high school in America by year-end 2000.

Based on the belief that it is God's will for every teenager to understand the gospel, the Challenge 2000 Alliance challenges you to join us in accomplishing this goal of a ministry to every school by the end of the year 2000.

Will You Adopt a School for Christ?

Prayerfully ask God what he would have you do to help communicate the gospel to every teenager in your area. Consider your part in making an impact through students at their nearby schools. If you have a plan for outreach, training, and prayer, please register the school you are targeting on the Challenge 2000 Web site: www.everyschool.com. Even if you are only able to pray, let us know which school you are claiming. Either log on the above Web site, or write us at Challenge 2000, c/o National Network of Youth Ministries, 12335 World Trade Drive #16, San Diego, CA, 92128.

Essential prayer and evangelism resources to equip teenagers and youth workers in reaching young people for Christ are available from The Challenge 2000 "Adopt A School" warehouse. Call 1-800-729-4716 to order or go on-line to: www.challenge2000.org.

If you can only order one thing, order The Starter Kit for Campus

Ministry. Though it is very inexpensive ($1.50 each), this is the most comprehensive and helpful tool for campus ministry available today. Everyone working with youth and every committed Christian teenager should have one. Highlights are:

▸ The Challenge 2000 Covenant wall poster and prayer triplet card.

▸ The Every School Plan, which offers a principle-driven, practical way of working with students at school.

▸ Information on how to do a Challenge 2000 service in your church, to commission students as campus missionaries.

▸ A catalog of more than 300 campus ministry resources from more than forty publishers.

▸ Prayer strategies, tips for starting campus Christian clubs, Bible study outlines, legal help, adult worker guidelines, and much more.

Consider Joining the National Network

Another way to keep abreast of the latest developments and resources of the Challenge 2000 Alliance is to join the organization that sponsors the alliance. There are a host of other benefits and the cost is as low as $39. Or you can have a free three-month trial membership. Call 1-800-FOR-NNYM or go online: www.nnym.org.

As illustrated by the recent campus shootings, people are realizing that American secondary schools are also one of the world's most needy mission fields. "Missionaries" are desperately needed. Adults can provide important support to this effort, but the actual missionaries must be the students themselves.

It is time for us to respond to God's call to reach students on campus. We must pray for and support ministries to reach teenagers if we ever hope to see awakening come to our neighborhoods, our cities, and our nation.

Paul Fleischmann is executive director, National Network of Youth Ministries and chairman, Challenge 2000 Alliance.

Twenty-Two

Y2K: A Lighthouse Opportunity

—SHAUNTI FELDHAHN—

Now I will rescue you and make you both a symbol and a source of blessing! So don't be afraid or discouraged, but instead get on with rebuilding the temple!

ZECHARIAH 8:13 (NLT)

As we approach the turn of the century, many people have become keenly interested in the unique problem known as the "year 2000 computer bug" or "Y2K." The problem is that some portion of our computing technology may stop functioning properly if it is not reprogrammed to recognize the next century, causing an unknown degree of disruption.

There is disagreement among even seasoned experts about whether Y2K will cause minor inconveniences or major turmoil in some sectors. At the very least, it is possible that there could be an economic downturn and a measure of technological disruption in our communities.

What many in the Christian community are beginning to realize, however, is that Y2K is more than just a technical problem: it is a unique ministry opportunity and responsibility. We as Christians must prepare our families, churches, and communities for possible Y2K-related problems, so that we can both handle whatever does happen and be "salt and light" to our neighbors.

As lighthouse keepers, you have a unique and very important role to play during this time. Each lighthouse keeper has a heart to pray, care, and share in his or her community, and meeting your neighbors is one of the most important linchpins in achieving that goal. Y2K may present some neighborhood needs that require a caring Christian response, and it may provide you with several ways to meet your neighbors in the first place.

Here is just one example of how this might work. Suppose you throw a block party and invite all the neighbors within your subdivision to watch a balanced Y2K video (such as "Y2K Investigative Report") and talk about what, if anything, the neighborhood wants to do to prepare. As you meet quite a few neighbors for the first time, you discover another Christian family one street over, as well as several other families who might be at higher risk of Y2K disruptions. For example, there are the two single moms struggling to make ends meet right now, during a good job market. There is the family with the disabled child requiring specialized medical equipment. Then there are the three senior citizens who depend on dicey pensions. And, of course, all the families would face difficulties if any essential services—such as power or water—were disrupted.

You and a few neighbors quietly set aside water, agree to establish a neighborhood watch, and otherwise take action to bring the community together. Real friendships are forged, and as you begin to care more about one another, you naturally look out for each other when and if Y2K difficulties emerge.

Most importantly, as several neighbors are shaken by the difficulties that have arisen, they realize that they are not as in control of their lives as they thought and begin to bring up God in their conversations with you. Through a seemingly absurd technical problem, our sovereign Lord has just given you the chance to pray, to care, and to share what is most important with those around you.

Next Steps

Y2K opportunities and responsibilities run deep for you as a Christian light in your neighborhood, and this chapter can only scratch the surface. These three steps will help you explore and implement the many ideas for how God can use you in this area:

1. Educate yourself about Y2K and specific strategies to care for your community. Here are some resources:

►My book, Y2K: *The Millennium Bug—A Balanced Christian Response* (Multnomah).

►The book *Y2K for Women,* by Karen Anderson (Thomas Nelson).

►The book *Salt and Light @ The Zero Hour,* by Drs. Mark and Betsy Neuenschwander (Regal).

►My monthly Y2K ministry newsletter (Multnomah), *Countdown Y2K.* (1-888-474-4Y2K)

►The video and companion Christian booklet "Y2K Investigative Report" (1-800-940-2447).

2. Prepare yourself for Y2K. Pray about what God would have you do given the unique situation of your family and neighborhood. Preparation should be physical, financial, and spiritual. Some starting points:

►Physical. Consider setting aside important items that might be hard to get if there are disruptions in local infrastructure or distribution channels, or if there is "panic buying" around the year-end. For example, food and other supplies, drinkable water (deemed particularly important by Y2K analysts), medicines, a little cash, and other items. Don't just do this for yourself. As a lighthouse, consider the possible needs of your neighbors as well.

►Financial. Biblical financial principles will withstand both good times and bad, so as much as is possible, stick to a budget, try to be out of debt, be diversified, have some savings, and continue to tithe.

3. Consider joining the Joseph Project 2000 network. This is a national nonprofit Christian network of individuals, churches, and ministries that are preparing for service and witness, as well as to be a public voice for God-honoring calm faith, during any economic downturn, Y2K-type disruptions, or other community hardship. To find out more about the Joseph Project, check out the Web site at www.josephproject2000.org.

Shaunti Feldhahn is founder and president of the Joseph Project 2000, a nonprofit organization devoted to Christian Y2K leadership. She is author of Y2K: The Millennium Bug—A Balanced Christian Response *(Multnomah)*

Twenty-Three

D-Day for Revival?

—Dale Schlafer—

For I will pour water on the thirsty land, and streams on the dry ground; I will pour out my Spirit on your offspring, and my blessing on your descendants.

Isaiah 44:3

January 22, 1999 may go down as a date that is as important to the history of the United States as was June 6, 1944. In 1944 the Allies landed on the beaches of Normandy in one of the greatest displays of military unity the world had ever seen. With that successful landing, the war was, for all intents and purposes, over. On January 22, in an unprecedented show of unity, denominations and servant ministries joined together to call the church in America to extraordinary prayer and fasting in a National Prayer Accord.

Mission America, a coalition made up of 71 denominations comprising almost 200,000 churches, 200 servant ministries, and 57 national ministry networks, called this meeting. Why? There is a growing realization that something is desperately wrong with the church of Jesus Christ in America. Revival is needed!

Clearly, God decides when revival fires come. But as a student of revival, I am deeply excited. This call represents a large portion of the church crying out for revival and awakening. When one looks at the history of revival it is obvious that revival comes in answer to prayer. And who sets the church to praying? It is God himself. If God is stirring the church to pray, then how can we believe anything else but that revival is on the way? He is calling his church—and you as a lighthouse—to pray!

Jonathan Edwards led a prayer effort that God used to usher in the First Great Awakening (1734-1750). Edwards read a treatise on united prayer for revival that had come from Scotland. This so stirred him that he expanded it and wrote his own work entitled, in typical Puritan style, "A Humble Attempt to Promote Explicit Agreement and Visible Union of All God's People in Extraordinary Prayer for Revival of Religion and Extension of Christ's Kingdom Throughout the Earth." This was Edwards's call to Christians, and the church everywhere, to unite in a workable strategy of synchronized prayer.

This strategy is better known as a "concert of prayer." Edwards expected this idea to spread quickly to the church in New England. All Christians, regardless of denomination, easily agreed upon the two prayer concerns: 1) revival of the church and 2) awakening of the lost. It spread quickly. By any measurement, it was united prayer and fasting that moved God to bring about the First Great Awakening.

In time, there was a great decline. God's people moved away from him once again. In fact, things got so bad that the Chief Justice of the United States Supreme Court, John Marshall, a concerned believer, said: "The Church is too far gone to ever be redeemed." Once again, God stirred the heart of a pastor, Isaac Backus, to realize the necessity of united prayer. As Edwards before him had done, he wrote a paper in 1794, entitled: "A Plea for Revival of Religion." He mailed it to pastors of every denomination in the United States, pleading for each man to set aside the first Monday of each month to open his church all day and conduct extraordinary prayer for revival. Almost every denomination joined in a call to their member churches imploring them to unite in prayer and fasting. Congregational, Baptist, Methodist, Presbyterians, and independents came together to pray. Then they prayed together within their cities or area. They crossed denominational barriers in the strength of unity to beseech God to bring the desperately needed revival. The answer to this united prayer and fasting became known as the Second Great Awakening (1794-1840).

No matter what revival and awakening you study, no matter where it took place or what transpired, you will usually find that passionate, persistent prayer is the key to revival. In the great awakening in China (1906–1908), it was prayer that moved God to bring revival. Jonathan Goforth, in his recounting of what took place, recorded one missionary saying: "There is no secret to revival. Revival always comes in answer to prayer."

J. Edwin Orr was fond of saying, "When God is about to do something he sets his people to praying." Imagine, what could happen if a hundred thousand key lighthouse churches and 3 to 6 million neighborhood lighthouses join in one mighty chorus, beseeching God to bring revival and awakening. Do you think something might happen? I do! That's why I believe we experienced a spiritual D-Day on January 22, 1999. Will you carry this call for extraordinary prayer to your churches and to your family, friends, and neighbors? Then that which is not yet will soon become a reality: a revived church and a great awakening of the lost!

Dale Schlafer is national facilitator of Pastors/Revival and Awakening Mission America.

Twenty-Four

A Vision to Evangelize First Nations Tribes

—Russell Begaye (Navajo)—

I have other sheep that are not of this sheep pen.
I must bring them also. They too will listen to my voice,
and there shall be one flock and one shepherd.

John 10:16

"First Nations Tribes" is a term used to describe those people who inhabited North America before the coming of Columbus. It encompasses 530 federally recognized tribal groups and nearly 50 groups recognized only by their state governments. Most of these live on 220 American Indian reservations established by the government of the United States. Others live on lands allotted to individual members of certain tribes but is still considered trust land of the government. Most of these are found in states like Oklahoma, Montana, Alaska, and California. People living on allotted lands are not considered as being part of a reservation but as a "First Nations community."

"Light the Nations" is a strategy to establish a lighthouse of prayer on every reservation and in every First Nations community. The goal is to start 10,000 prayer houses and to pray for every home among the First Nations tribal groups.

Millions of mission dollars, thousands of man hours and several million pounds of food and clothing have been expended to evangelize the "Indian." Yet, less than 10 percent have become followers of Jesus. I am convinced that we have done everything to win First Nations tribes to Jesus Christ…except pray. The time is now for all First Nations followers of the Jesus way to become lighthouses of prayer for their communities on every reservation and First Nations communities.

Prayer is the voice of the deepest part of our being. It expresses our sorrow and joy, our remorse and love. The prayers for our First Nations tribes must come from those depths. They must go deeper than the mind, though that gives it guidance. They must be more than knowledge, though that gives pertinent information. They must go deeper than our tongues, though they provide the vehicle for its expression. Our prayers for our First Nations tribes must come from our rebirth spirit that has been infused with the love of our great Creator.

Three factors need to be considered as we look to make our prayers come alive. These factors are to be used as a guide but not to serve as a deterrent, obstacle, or excuse to presenting the gospel to First Nations people.

▸**Culture.** Native Americans have a wide variety of cultural expressions, origins, and traditions. With the influence of foreign settlers, these cultural expressions and traditions have been constantly modified since the 1600s. Today, there are traditional and nontraditional Native Americans. Traditional Native Americans are recognized by their language usage, cultural practices, and teachings that define their outlook on life. Most live in the West, where reservations are more isolated from outside influences. Nontraditional Native Americans are very diverse. Education and contact with the dominant surrounding culture have contributed to the varying degrees of assimilation that are found among this group.

▸**Family.** Today's First Nations families can be divided into three distinct groups. First are the nuclear families, which have close ties with their cultural ways and customs and maintain relationships with relatives. They seek cultural and social support from tribal members. Second are the acculturated families, which are one step removed from their tribal heritage. Their contact and dependence on the cultural is lessened. They develop cross-cultural friendship with members of other tribal groups and non-First Nations families. Their affinity to their heritage and knowledge of their culture is minimized. Third are the marginalized families, which have a modified perception of their culture that is different than that of the nuclear families. Most of these do not speak their tribal language. Value is placed on success more than maintaining cultural distinctives. For these families obtaining a good education and employment is a priority.

▸**Religion.** Tribal religion is so closely tied to tribal culture that it presents unique challenges in the area of evangelism. Many tribal members will interpret Christian evangelistic efforts to mean that they must give up the heritage that is so sacred to them. In other words, most tribal people believe they have to stop being First Nations people in order to be a Christian. Because of this misconception, the gospel message is often met with a cold reception.

The most important question when considering praying for First Nations people is, "How do you begin?" Start with your neighborhood. Begin praying for five houses located to the right and left of you. On some reservations the fifth house may be five miles down the road. Pray for that house each time you drive by. Second, begin to find ways to minister to the people you are praying for. Look for opportunities to minister. Third, ask God to give you an opportunity to verbally share the Good News of Jesus Christ with the people you are praying for.

If you live in a First Nations community but your immediate neighbors are non-First Nations tribal members, locate a lighthouse of prayer located in a predominant First Nations neighborhood and become a prayer partner. You will need to meet with this lighthouse of prayer on a regular basis.

If you are a non-First Nations member and do not live on a reservation or in a First Nations community, contact me at rbegaye9@idt.net for an assignment, or visit the First Nations Forum's Web-site at http://www.angelfire.com/ok2/LightTheNations.

Russell Begaye is manager and national multiethnic specialist of North American Mission Board.

Twenty-Five

Urban Lighthouses

—Dr. John M. Perkins—

The righteous care about justice for the poor,
but the wicked have no such concern.

Proverbs 29:7

Questions are being asked from every sector of American society about the direction we should head as a nation. Everyone from powerful politicians to the average person on the street seems to be confused about solutions for our declining inner cities.

Thirty years after the successes of the Civil Rights Movement of the fifties and sixties, we stand at another crossroads. The civil rights era was probably the most important social movement of this century and the voting rights legislation that accompanied it brought the black community into full citizenship. Poverty and affirmative action programs did much to create a large and thriving middle class, and minority elected officials are at an all-time high. Much progress has been made.

But at the same time that all this progress was being made, a new phenomenon was developing. This phenomenon has been dubbed the "underclass." This stubborn new form of poverty is a by-product of black economic and political/legislative success, well-intentioned poverty programs gone awry, and, of course, the persistence of racism.

There is still much unfinished business. The moral crisis we face in this country is crying out for spiritual leadership. It offers evangelicals the opportunity to put our faith to work—to become players instead of sitting on the sidelines. It offers many of us opportunities to be what I call urban lighthouses.

The John M. Perkins Foundation is currently working on a project that grew out of the untimely death of my eldest son, Spencer Perkins, in January 1998. His vision was to see all races working together, unified by the gospel of Christ in carrying out God's work here on earth. In memory of our son, my wife, Vera Mae, and I decided to develop the Spencer Perkins Center for Reconciliation and Youth Development, a training facility that will represent Spencer and what his life meant to us as well as others around the country. Our aim is to reach children, beginning at the age of four—Spencer's age when he began to follow Christ. It is imperative that a new generation of young people is raised up who will reach out to our hurting loved ones. Our goal is to train urban leaders to love and express God's love to young people as they grow up, and before they get into trouble.

We will build this center with volunteer labor and with the financial assistant of our supporters and friends. I invite you to join us, individually or with a work group. The skills in the various work groups vary, but anyone with any skill—or no skills—can be put to a task.

There are already signs that the evangelical community, which has been faithful in preaching a bold message of salvation but long silent on social issues like poverty and race, is beginning to make its presence felt. I am encouraged by what I see happening in movements across the country. Almost everyplace I go, there is a spark of renewal. David Bryant's Concert of Prayer is very active, and I'm greatly encouraged by Promise Keepers, the men's movement that was started by Bill McCartney, and by Mission America, led by my dear friend Paul Cedar.

InterVarsity has been doing some wonderful work with their urban projects, reaching minorities, especially Asians. InterVarsity has developed a marketplace ministry led heavily by Pete Hammon and his staff.

Campus Crusade, a movement started by Dr. Bill Bright many years ago to reach out to high school and college students, is now the largest mission organization in the world. Out of this movement is blossoming an effort to reach urban children, headed by Dan Pryor, called SAY (Save America's Youth) Yes. Dan is working with churches to make their facilities and resources available for after-school tutoring programs.

Also, the Christian Community Development Association (CCDA), led by Wayne Gordon and myself, with a wonderful board of directors, has become the place for Christians who are working in our most forgotten communities taking the vision of Christian community development and racial reconciliation back to the streets.

CCDA is an association of like-minded Christian churches, ministries, families, schools, businesses, and individuals who are engaged in a variety of activities—from evangelism to housing, from health care to youth development, from homeless shelters to creating jobs. The membership of CCDA is multiracial and the leaders of its member ministries are heavily drawn from America's minority communities.

Whether you have been working in the trenches for years, or wondering how to get started, or simply have a concern to see God's love made visible among the poor, you can join the people of CCDA as we strive to be obedient to Jesus' mandate to bring his healing gospel to the poor and captive.

For information on CCDA membership services, including our annual conference, regional conferences, newsletters, employment opportunities, or other resources, write the Christian Community Development Association at 3827 West Ogden Ave., Chicago, Ill. 60623, or call 773-762-0994 (fax: 773-762-5772), or log onto CCDA on-line at www.ccda.org. Our E-mail address is CHICCDA@aol.com.

To purchase these books on urban community restoration, you may contact CCDA or write the John M. Perkins Foundation for Reconciliation and Development, 1831 Robinson St., Jackson, MS 39209. Phone: 601-354-1563, Fax: 601-352-6882, E-mail: jmpfoffice@aol.com.

Dr. John M. Perkins is founder of Christian Community Development Corporation.

Twenty-Six

Shining the Light across Language Boundaries

—JESSE MIRANDA AND THOMAS WANG—

When they heard this sound, a crowd came together in bewilderment, because each one heard them speaking in his own language.

ACTS 2:6

Nautical lighthouses are located in areas where there is potential danger. They shine in many places and come in many designs, but their mission is always the same: to warn of peril. Lighthouses exist to help ships' captains and crew avoid shipwrecks. They warn sailors of danger, and they do so without regard to a captain's or a crew's race, creed, or language.

In similar fashion, Mission America's lighthouse prayer and outreach ministries are designed to meet the spiritual needs of the diverse population of America and to prevent spiritual shipwrecks. We believe they are a movement of God to place people on the path of his grace. Like nautical lighthouses, they accomplish their mission without regard to race, creed, or language.

We want to introduce the Lighthouse Movement to those who speak languages other than English. Language has never been, and should never be, an obstacle to the spread of the gospel or a barrier to the work of God among the people of this nation. If darkness is penetrated among all people and in many languages—and it most certainly is—so must the light of Jesus Christ shine among all people and in many languages.

Jesus said, "I am the light of the world. Whoever follows me will never walk in darkness, but will have the light of life" (John 8:12). He shares this light with his followers as he said, "You are the light of the world. A city on a hill cannot be hidden" (Matthew 5:14).

The light of which our Lord spoke is not an idea or a program, but God's people in action doing good works. Our burgeoning cities are made up of people of all ethnic groups and cultures, speaking all different languages and dialects, and these people should not be hidden in darkness but brought in the light by the multiplied works of all believers.

Although we as the followers of Jesus do not "walk in darkness," we must walk through the darkness with our light. The light (and salt) factor is God's strategy to spread the Good News and its influence to a corrupt and dark world. That is why he has left us here on earth…to make certain that all have a chance to see the light of God shining from us.

We encourage followers of Christ of all different languages—including English and all its dialects—to work to complete the task of shining our light, using godly actions and words, into every corner of our society where darkness exists.

Millions want to hear in their own language the Good News of the gospel. How can this be done? By speakers of different languages joining the millions of other lighthouse keepers and strategically establish a lighthouse in their neighborhood. A lighthouse is a place in a community—a house, a place of business, or a church—that shines the light in the midst of darkness. A lighthouse keeper is one who prays, cares, and gives what it takes to shine the light, including the use of other languages.

Bilingual persons in particular can become effective—not to mention vital—lighthouse keepers to bridge the language gaps that may exist. We encourage you to utilize your gift to let others know of the grace of God. Let us not leave a single dark corner without the glimmer of hope that comes with the light of the gospel.

Make friends!
Solicit prayer requests!
Pray fervently and purposefully!
Plan evangelism initiatives!
Build links with the Body of Christ.

And if God has put you in a place where others who speak different languages can see your light shine, use your ability to speak their language to make certain that they have every opportunity to hear the gospel of Christ.

Jesse Miranda is president of AMEN. Thomas Wang is president of Great Commission Fellowship, International.

Twenty-Seven

From the Jews, for the Jews

—Moishe Rosen—

For there is no difference between Jew and Gentile—the same Lord is Lord of all and richly blesses all who call on him, for, "Everyone who calls on the name of the Lord will be saved."

Romans 10:12–13

The temple Solomon built was God's lighthouse for all peoples, but the lighthouse at Jerusalem flickered and went out. Yet through the millennia and centuries, the Lord has been whispering to a yet-future Israel: "Arise, shine; for your light has come. And the glory of the Lord rises upon you" (Isaiah 60:1).

That glory arrived as the person of Jesus Christ, who was the promised Messiah. But the darkness crowded into the hearts of men. The darkness tried to vanquish the light of the Messiah, only to find that the Light they thought could be extinguished came back to ignite thousands and millions of flickering lights around the world. Yet Israel as a nation is blinded in part to his light (Romans 11:25). It is up to the church to be a lighthouse to Israel, the Jewish people.

One reason to evangelize the Jews is that in Christ, Jews find the meaning of the Jewish destiny. Jews have been longing for what they know not and cannot recognize. But Jews are finding Christ, and for us it is like coming home. In Christ we realize that all the suffering and rejection has meaning. Does the church not owe a debt to bring the gospel message to those who first brought the message to the nations?

Jews are zealous Christians. A Jew who has endured the rejection of his kin and friends for Christ's sake is perhaps even more ready to bear witness to the unsaved peoples of all nations. He knows that what he has gained in Christ and the church family is far more than any affection or popularity that the world might withhold because of his testimony. Because a Jew must be willing to be an outcast to come to faith in Christ, he is not so easily manipulated into silence by the offense that others might take.

There are only 12.5 million Jews in the world today. Yet the influence and impact of the Jewish people are well beyond their proportional numbers. In the field of medicine the Jewish contribution to civilization is great. In the field of music we have a Leonard Bernstein, Harold Arlen, or Bob Dylan. See how many Pulitzer Prize or Nobel Peace Prize winners are Jewish (*What the Church Owes the Jew,* Leslie Flynn, 1998).

God used the Jewish race to produce an Albert Einstein, a Jonas Salk, but most of all Abraham, Moses, and Jesus. But then why shouldn't the Jewish people have great influence? They are the people God chose to be the prophetic race, the people God used to write the Bible.

Not all Christians can say with the apostle Paul, "For I am not ashamed of the gospel of Christ, for it is the power of God to salvation for everyone who believes, for the Jew first and also for the Greek" (Romans 1:16, NKJV). Christians usually have no trouble in telling of the salvation that can be found in Christ to those who already know and respect the Bible. Yet Christians often cower when confronted by a Jew who might take offense at the gospel.

But that need not be so. Any Christian can effectively witness to Jews if he recognizes that it is not up to him as an individual Christian to convert his Jewish friend. His duty is only to proclaim the gospel, to sow the gospel seed. The Holy Spirit will see that the seed is watered and grows, and perhaps another Christian might be the harvester. People respond by hearing, reading, or seeing many small things that serve to impress them toward the Lord. It is up to us to sow many seeds of impression.

Some of the Things That Must Be Remembered in Witnessing to Jews:

1. When a Jew accepts Jesus, he doesn't stop being Jewish. He becomes a Christian but not a Gentile. Jews have been taught that they must retain their Jewishness, and even God himself emphasized that. So if they receive Christ they are still Jews in God's sight. "Jewish" and "Christian" as terms applied to people are not mutually exclusive categories. All of the early followers of Jesus were 100 percent Jewish and 100 percent Christian. Jewish people are indoctrinated to believe they must be Jewish, and most Jews do not follow Judaism; that is, the religion originated by the rabbis.

2. Jews are saved like anyone else: by faith in Christ. Even though they are the chosen people, the promises to Israel are earthly promises, not heavenly ones. The salvation that Christ offers is the salvation from sin and unto eternal life.

3. In the Jewish religion, there is very little said about sin, the Savior, and salvation, and these need to be effectively explained.

4. In witnessing to Jews, don't to try to move them to confess Christ before you have made an adequate presentation of the gospel.

5. Contrary to popular thought, it is not necessary to restrict your witness to the Old Testament. Most Jews have very little knowledge of the Bible and don't trust themselves to make decisions based on the Bible. However, the Holy Spirit is the great persuader, and just the very person of Jesus is attractive.

6. Remember the essential character of Christianity is Jewishness fulfilled. (For those wanting more information, see my book *Witnessing to Jews*, Purple Pomegranate Productions, 1998.)

Evangelizing Jewish people is not nearly as difficult as people have found in the past. In these last days, God seems to be doing a work among the Jews.

For those wanting more information on resources, contact:

Jews for Jesus
60 Haight St., San Francisco CA 94102
415-552-8325 Fax
Jews4Jesus@aol.com
http://www.jewsforjesus.org

Moishe Rosen is founder of Jews For Jesus.

Twenty-Eight

Prayer Resources & Opportunities

—EDDIE SMITH—

When I heard these things, I sat down and wept. For some days I mourned and fasted and prayed before the God of heaven.

NEHEMIAH 1:4

Welcome to the ministry of prayer mobilization! As you enter into this ministry, keep in mind that you are a minister unto the Lord. Not only that, yours is the ministry that is closest to God's heart. Not only did prayer permeate Jesus' earthly life, but today he intercedes for us continually at the right hand of the Father in heaven (see Hebrews 7:25). Not only are prayer and worship closest to God's heart, they are the only ministry opportunities one can find in heaven!

Prayer is so much on God's heart that he said his church would become a "house of prayer." And around the world today churches are becoming houses of prayer, and homes are becoming lighthouses of prayer, as the greatest prayer movement is history is occurring. Dr. C. Peter Wagner, world-renowned missiologist and prayer leader says, "The worldwide prayer movement is out of control!"

If you're like I was in 1993, when I entered the prayer ministry, you are still trying to figure out what God is up to. It took me an entire year to begin to see the picture.

Here is the list of the top ten prayer initiatives that take place each year. I have included brief descriptions of each, plus information on how to take part:

▸ **First Friday Fasting and Prayer** (monthly)—This is a day of fasting and prayer one day each month for revival and for those in authority (1 Timothy 2:1).

Information
Phone: 1-800-USA PRAY (872-7729)
Web site: www.ifa-usapray.org
E-mail: usapray@aol.com

▸ **Thirty-Day Muslim Prayer Focus** (During Ramadan, the Muslim month of prayer)—Calling the church to pray for the Muslim world.

Information
Phone: 719-380-0507
Web site: www.ywam.com
E-mail: wcn30days@aol.com

▸ **PrayUSA!** (Ash Wednesday through Palm Sunday [Lent])—Forty days of prayer and fasting for revival and spiritual awakening in the U.S. A Mission America/Celebrate Jesus prayer initiative coordinated by the U.S. PRAYER TRACK.

Information
Phone: 713-466-4009
Fax-on-Demand: 713-466-6392, Doc. #200
Web site: www.prayusa.com
E-mail: 75711.2501@compuserve.com
(Kits available beginning January 1 each year by calling 888-531-3379)

▸ **National Day of Prayer** (First Thursday in May)—A day for personal and corporate prayer and repentance, particularly on behalf of our nation and those in leadership.

Information

Phone: 719-531-3379 (Kits available)

▸ **Nationally Televised Concert of Prayer** (First Thursday evening in May)—A concert of prayer links America's spiritual leaders to thousands of Christians by satellite in repentance and prayer for revival and spiritual awakening.

Information

Phone: 612-853-1758

E-mail: LaurieSeay@compuserve.com

▸ **March for Jesus/Jesus Day**—A day to mobilize the church to fill each community with demonstrations of God's love. The intent is to encourage ongoing community ministry by the body of Christ linking spiritual passion with social action.

Information

Phone: 512-416-0066

Web site: www.mfj.org

E-mail: mfjusa@compuserve.com

▸ **"See You at the Pole"** (September)—Elementary, junior high, senior high, and college students gather around their school flagpoles before classes begin to pray for their unsaved classmates, their faculty, and anything that is on their hearts.

Information

Phone: 619-592-9200

Web site: www.syatp.com

E-mail: info@syatp.com

▸ **National Concert of Prayer Rallies** (October)—An annual event linking concerts of prayer in communities across the nation where Christians gather to pray for spiritual awakening and revival in their communities, our nation, and the world.

Information:
Phone: 512-416-0066
Web site: www.mfj.org
E-mail: mfjusa@compuserve.com

▸ **Fasting & Prayer** (November)—A gathering of Christian leaders linked by satellite TV to more than one million Christians worldwide who are humbling themselves, fasting, repenting, and praying for revival and spiritual awakening.

Information
Phone: 800-888-FAST (3278)
Web site: www.fastingprayer.com

▸ **International Day of Prayer for the Persecuted Church**—Christians around the world suffer in silence. It's time the church received compelling information, offered regular prayer, and too appropriate action on their behalf.

Information:
Phone: 847-718-0560
Web site: www.persecutedchurch.org
E-mail: idop@xc.org

With these national and international initiatives there are literally hundreds of more local and regional initiatives. Truly, the prayer movement is "out of control!"

There are other resources with which you should be familiar. I suggest you call them and ask for their catalog or product information:

▸ **Pray!** magazine (bimonthly)—A magazine published by The Navigators to challenge and equip believers to pray more diligently and effectively; to encourage believers to step out of their comfort zones in regard to prayer; and to inform believers of the scope of the prayer movement and its organizations. For a free copy or to subscribe, call 800-691-7729. See the Web site at www.praymag.com or e-mail at pray.mag@navpress.com.

▸ **PrayerNet Newsletter** (biweekly)—Free E-mail newsletter on prayer and revival. E-mail at 75711.2501@compuserve.com with the message "subscribe."

▸ **UpLink** (monthly)—Free, monthly newsletter on prayer and revival. To subscribe, call 713-466-4009.

▸ **America's National Prayer** Committee's Web site for Lighthouses of Prayer—See site at www.nationalprayer.org/lighthouse.html.

▸ **The U.S. PRAYER TRACK's** Web site—For teaching and prayer resources. See site at www.usprayertrack.org.

▸ **Prayer Audio** magazine (monthly)—Twelve monthly cassettes featuring the world's foremost authorities on prayer. Call 1-800-597-1123 for more information.

▸ **U.S. Prayer Directory**—If you would like to be listed at no charge, or to receive a copy of the U.S. Prayer Directory with the names and contact information of hundreds of other prayer ministries and ministry leaders on computer disk call 713-466-4009.

May the Father's prayer anointing rest upon your life. May he give you favor with leadership as well as with those you are to lead. And may he fill your lighthouse of prayer with joy!

Eddie Smith is co-coordinator of U.S. PRAYER TRACK.

Twenty-Nine

Lighthouses of Reconciliation

—DR. RALEIGH WASHINGTON—

Leave your gift there in front of the altar. First go and be reconciled to your brother; then come and offer your gift.

MATTHEW 5:24

It is my personal conviction that the fullness of revival in America will not take place without reflecting a clear and unmistakable picture of the God-created diversity of the body of Christ in our country.

Current research reveals that America is undergoing a population shift. Numerous reports indicate that in thirty-five to forty years, white Americans will no longer be in the majority. On Friday, April 11, 1997, President Clinton stated, "It is really potentially a great thing for America that we are becoming so multiethnic at the time the world is becoming so closely tied together. But it's also a powder keg of problems and heartbreak and division and loss." He added, "How we handle it...may be the biggest single determinant of what we look like fifty years from now and what our position in the world is." He also issued a challenge to "Get to know people who are your age, but who are different than you—people of a different racial or ethnic group, people of a different religion—because you are going to live in the most multiethnic, multiracial, multireligious democracy in human history" (Centre Daily Times [communities of central Pennsylvania], Saturday, April 12, 1997).

Considering this, it is even more critical that the Lighthouse Movement will encompass all races and denominations. Specifically, it is our hope that many individual lighthouses will take the extra step of being reconcilers in their cities by partnering with a lighthouse that is denominationally and racially different from themselves. As a result, the peace, blessing, and the light of the gospel will reach the lost all across this land.

At Promise Keepers, reconciliation is an integral part of the ministry. We believe the Seven Promises can be lived out according to "Eight Biblical Principles of Reconciliation," which apply to all relationships, particularly in diverse situations. Applying them to lighthouses will enhance the movement's effectiveness by inviting more people to commit to be lighthouses, increasing the diversity and improving the relationships of those participating lighthouses.

Eight Principles of Reconciliation

1. The Call (2 Corinthians 5:17–21). While some have a special gift in ministering in diverse situations, we are all called to be involved in the ministry of reconciliation.

2. Commitment to Relationship (Ruth 1:16–17). Relationship is the foundation of reconciliation. Commitment suggests an element of permanency to the bond—and that relentless effort put into resolving any conflicts that may arise. Lighthouse participants must see every new relationship made as permanent rather than temporary.

3. Intentionality (Ephesians 2:14–15). To be intentional, lighthouses that practice reconciliation must be purposeful, positive, and planned in their approach. "Intentionality" suggests that each lighthouse should seek to involve people who represent the diversity that is inherent to our nation. In addition to neighbors, target the local policeman, mailman, professor, garbageman, businessman, yardman, bus driver, pastor, custodian, and the parent of that team member of your son's football team who is a different race than you.

4. Sincerity (John 15:15). The principle of sincerity demands that during lighthouse communications, you choose to be vulnerable, disclosing your feelings, attitudes, and perceptions with the goal of relating meaningfully to your neighbor. Sincerity is a prerequisite for building trust.

5. Sensitivity (Ephesians 4:15–16). Sensitivity is the intentional acquisition of knowledge in order to relate to any diverse situation, person, place, or organization. A helpful phrase to use in lighthouse communications is "Help me understand." Most people are eager to be understood. Saying this often opens a door to receiving a prayer request.

6. Sacrifice (Philippians 2:3–4). Sacrifice reminds us that no relationship is established without a cost. For instance, the first thing I enjoy doing when I get home each day is watching the news. Sacrifice may demand that I give that up so that I can go for a prayer walk in my neighborhood. Intentionally choosing to step out of our homogenous comfort zones will yield a multitude of blessings.

7. Empowerment (2 Corinthians 8:9). Repentance and forgiveness will create and maintain an atmosphere of grace, thus empowering relationships. If you are found to be at fault in a relationship, immediately repent. If you are harboring ill will against another, forgive him. If you do these things, the atmosphere for ministry will be established. This is especially critical to reach across diverse barriers successfully.

8. Interdependence (2 Corinthians 8:12–14). With our varying gifts and interests, almighty God has created each of us with a unique ability to contribute to others something they do not have. In addition, interdependence engenders humility, which is a powerful ingredient for making friends.

Incorporation of the principles described in this chapter will equip and empower you to reach across diverse relational barriers, greatly enhancing the effectiveness of your lighthouse.

Dr. Raleigh Washington is the vice president of reconciliation at Promise Keepers and has authored a reconciliation training guide, Break Down the Walls Workbook, *with Glen Kehrein and Claude V. King. For fifteen years, he served as the pastor of a multiracial congregation at Rock Evangelical Free Church in Chicago.*

Thirty

Diverse Lighthouses

—Dr. Tom Phillips—

For my house will be called a house of prayer for all nations.

Isaiah 56:7

I believe that prayer is foundational to everything we do for God, and I believe God will open the windows of heaven on this nation as we pray.

An article I recently read stated that the crime rate is coming down throughout our nation. I think it's due to all the prayer that's going on for our neighborhoods, for our cities, and, indeed, for our entire nation.

Many of us, when we think of lighthouses of prayer, think of those people who come together in homes across this nation to pray for their communities. But what about those communities that are different? College campuses are communities made up of souls who need prayer as much as those in your neighborhood. For example, each year 550,000 international students study at universities across our nation. The window of time they are here may be the only opportunity they have to hear the Good News of the gospel. What about our schools and the problems our youth face in these institutions that deny the existence of our God?

I'm sure you'll agree that we need to set up lighthouses to pray for these different communities around us.

In order to focus our prayer, it helps to have specific information about these different communities.

As you consider a commitment to pray for the students in our colleges and universities, don't forget the international students who study in the United States each year. International Students, Inc. (ISI) has a mission to reach these future leaders of the world with the gospel so that they in turn can bring home the Good News to share with their people. So strategic is this mission that we are growing a network of prayer warriors who will hold our ministry up in prayer on a regular basis. You can help ISI by contacting the International Student Lighthouse of Prayer to receive more information about how to pray for your local campus. Call 1-800-474-8326, and if you'd like to learn more about ISI's ministry, or check out our Web site at: www.isionline.org.

Another example is Campus Renewal Ministries, which plans to set up 10,000 lighthouses of prayer in the spring of 1999. All 10,000 lighthouses will be operating by the end of the next school year. These lighthouses will be located on and around college and university campuses across the nation. Students will pray for those who live around them in their dorms, apartment complexes, and fraternity and sorority houses. These lighthouses provide a unique opportunity for the churches and parachurch groups involved with each campus to work together to share the love of Jesus with students. Campus Renewal Ministries has developed a kit that helps set up and strengthen collegiate lighthouses. The kit includes CDs, booklets, door hangers, and more. You can order a kit by calling toll free 1-888-PRAYKIT.

Christian Camping International/USA (CCI/USA) is an association of nearly 1,000 camps, conference centers, and retreat centers mainly across the United States. Every year, more than five and a half million people participate in programs put on by members of CCI/USA, and about 268,000 come to faith in Jesus Christ through that experience. Concerted prayer for those camp attendees can make a difference. At ISI, we saw the results of focused prayer for a conference we held for Chinese students and scholars in 1997. Lives were changed during that one-week conference, and I believe the prayer that went on in preparation for the conference and during it released the power of God to work in the lives of those students and scholars. For more information about the Christian camps and conferences going on around you tap into CCI/USA's home page at www.cciusa.org.

Why not add to your list of those for whom you pray the schools in your neighborhood? For specific information about how to pray for your schools, contact the Christian Educators Association International. CEAI is a professional organization of Christian teachers, educators, principals, administrators, and other personnel whose goal is to ensure that children receive a quality academic education that is solidly connected to moral and spiritual values. Contact CEAI by calling (888) 798-1124 or by E-mailing info@ceai.org. You can also learn more about CEAI by checking out their Web site at www.ceai.org.

There are many more communities that need prayer—from nursing homes to our nations' prisons. You're already making a difference in your own neighborhoods, so why not consider being a lighthouse to the "different communities" where you live?

Dr. Tom Phillips is president/CEO of International Students, Inc.

Thirty-One

Christian Stores Provide Fuel for Lighthouses

—BILL ANDERSON—

Finally, brothers, whatever is true, whatever is noble, whatever is right, whatever is pure, whatever is lovely, whatever is admirable—if anything is excellent or praiseworthy—think about such things.

PHILIPPIANS 4:8

In the past decade, even our consumer-driven society has become increasingly conscious of what we put in our bodies. We're preoccupied with nutritional charts, calorie consumption, and water purity. We understand that what we consume affects our health and well-being.

The adage "You are what you eat" also applies to matters of the heart and mind. What we "consume" dramatically affects our spiritual walk and effectiveness. It matters what we think about, read, listen to, and watch. It matters because "What Goes Into the Mind Comes Out in a Life."

The Bible urges repeatedly: "Impress [the commandments] on your children. Talk about them when you sit at home and when you walk along the road" (Deuteronomy 6:7); "Meditate in [the law] day and night" (Joshua 1:8); "Finally, brothers, whatever is true, whatever is noble, whatever is right, whatever is pure, whatever is lovely, whatever is admirable —if anything is excellent or praiseworthy—think about such things." (Philippians 4:8).

You have a great resource near you to help in your personal growth, equip you for effective service, and assist you in ministry: a Christian retail store. A Christian bookstore... and more, really, a Christian lifestyle store.

It's a store of one book...the Bible. Christian products are tools to help us understand the Bible better, live in obedience, and share the gospel. Christian merchandise opens doors to express our love, worship, and commitment to Christ. Christian materials teach truth, build values, encourage faith, and shape lives. When people read Christian books, listen to Christian music, watch Christian videos, or enjoy Christian artwork, God's truth is at work—instilling something good in their minds that's sure to come out in speech and action.

God uses Christian products to extend your ministry effectiveness and help fulfill the Great Commission. A wealth of resources help believers understand what the Bible says about life's real issues, and also can be placed in the hands of that person we're ministering to—giving the Bible's unique perspective. "This book will help you in your desire to relate to your teenager; the author explains it all a lot better than I can. Let's read it and talk through it together." The people you care about have a variety of needs—building strong marriages and meaningful relationships, raising kids, developing character, and dealing with depression, loss, cancer, and death. The list goes on to virtually any subject people face.

We also need leisure and entertainment activity. Christian music, fiction, and videos offer positive alternatives based on God's truth. Entertainment that builds up the life, rather than tearing down values.

Jesus used storytelling as a teaching tool. A busy mom can choose a video that gives her six-year-old not only entertainment but also instruction through stories that teach moral values—developing fundamental character qualities. It seems now that teenagers can't do homework without headsets, and Christian lyrics reinforce biblical values. The entertainment of Christian fiction provides adventure and romance...without coarse language and explicit descriptions.

Christian stores also provide in-depth study tools to help us dig deeper into God's Word—study Bibles, commentaries, reference works, and Bible software. Devotional, inspirational, and how-to-books can be found to nurture spiritual disciplines.

We're called to be salt and light. As a person interested in letting your light shine, you know the need to fuel your lighthouse and keep the windows clean so the light beams out without obstruction.

Christian stores are committed to serving Christ by serving you through their ministry. These stores are owned and staffed by dedicated individuals who care about people. Like pastors and missionaries, they sense a calling to this exciting ministry—which operates as a business in the open marketplace. Their method is retail. Their motive is ministry.

There are Christian storehouses with fuel for your lighthouse. They're ready to help you—offering Bibles, books, study materials, music, gifts, videos, software, witness wear, children's products, and more. To speak to a person at a Christian store near you call CBA's toll-free store-direct connect at 1-800-991-7747, or log onto www.christianstores.org.

Jesus was purposeful to see things from God's perspective. He was intentional about teaching God's values, perspective, and truth. He emphasized issues of the heart, thinking God's thoughts, obedience, and walking in fellowship.

I encourage you to take full advantage of the resources provided through Christian products—expressed in a variety of media and sensitive to age and spiritual-maturity levels, while being biblically based and culturally relevant. And that's important, because What Goes Into the Mind Comes Out in a Life.

Bill Anderson is president and CEO of Christian Booksellers Association.

Thirty-Two

Lighthouse Worship

—STEVEN FRY—

God is spirit, and his worshipers must worship in spirit and in truth.

JOHN 4:24

Many things can motivate us to reach out to others: the desire to see broken people mended, the ache to see our nation spiritually or morally rejuvenated, the impulse to resist darkness in every sector of our society. But the only motivation for ministry that lasts a lifetime is that which flows out of a passion for God.

How can we maintain such passion? How do we cultivate an intimate relationship with God? By worshiping him. The priority of worship is succinctly summarized in the mission statement of Integrity Music, a company that has produced some of the finest praise recordings in the country: "There is one thing on earth that we will continue to do in Heaven. That is to praise and worship God. That is why we view life on earth, for those who love Jesus, as choir practice for Heaven."

But why is worship so important to a lighthouse ministry? Here are five reasons:

1. All effective ministry flows out of an intimate relationship with

God, and that relationship is first and foremost cultivated through worshiping him. Unless we spend time waiting on God, allowing his Holy Spirit to create within us an appetite to know him, we will eventually lose our desire to share his love with others. We'll find that we're responding to God more out of duty than desire. Good works, unless they are fueled by a passion for God, can actually generate apathy and burnout.

2. Worshiping God is a primary key to knowing him. Isaiah was awe-struck by God's glory and the sound of fiery seraphs exclaiming "Holy, Holy, Holy, Lord God Almighty!" Think of it! These angelic creatures have repeated this refrain for millennia past counting! What could ever motivate creatures to worship so? Could it be that every time they worship, God reveals something of himself they have never seen? Oh, the knowledge of God is inexhaustible! Worship opens our heart to knowing him, and knowing him fuels our passion to make him known to others.

3. Worshiping God makes us sensitive to his prompting. That is why worship is intricately linked with prayer and intercession. Without meaning to, we can find ourselves praying our agenda, about things we feel are important. Yet, one of the great secrets to effective intercession is to understand God's thoughts about a given situation and pray accordingly. The Bible clearly says in Isaiah 55:8 that God's ways are not our ways, neither are his thoughts our thoughts. We need to know his thoughts, and that kind of sensitivity is cultivated in worship.

4. Worship and praise sensitizes us to the presence of the kingdom of God. Remember, the kingdom really means Christ's rule. Wherever Jesus is in charge, the kingdom of God is manifest. In Psalm 22:3, we read that the Lord is "enthroned upon the praises of Israel." That passage is better understood, "The Lord's rulership is in effect wherever God's people praise him" (nasb). Just simply walking our streets, quietly singing God's praises can change the atmosphere of our neighborhoods. Over time, you will find people more receptive to the love of Jesus.

5. Worship and praise is often the way God garners the first fruits of the harvest. For example, 3,000 people were added to the church on that celebrated Pentecost day recorded in Acts 2. But was it due to the effective preaching of Peter alone? No, for Peter's inspired sermon came on the heels of an explosion of praise and worship. The Holy Spirit had filled the disciples, and they began to speak in other languages declaring the wonders of God. They were worshiping God! The curiosity of many was aroused, and Peter's sermon simply threw out the net to catch the fish.

How can we cultivate an enriching worship life? One model is found in Ezekiel 44, where God instructs a group of priests on their "ministry" to him. First, they would take off their wool garments and put on linen robes. For they were not to wear anything that made them sweat in God's presence (Ezekiel 44:17). Sometimes we can find ourselves "sweating" in our quiet times with God, our minds a whirlwind of demands and distractions. Yet we are to "Be still, and know that I am God" (Psalm 46:10). So, at the beginning of a praise time, take several moments in prayer to put all of those distractions in God's "pending" tray until you have "quieted yourself" before him. Then you can focus on him and worship with passion.

Second, listen to the promptings of the Holy Spirit. Jesus said to the woman at the well (John 4) that the Father seeks worshipers who will worship him in spirit and in truth. Begin to sing out the truths of God's character—his faithfulness, his power, his mercy. To worship in spirit is to be consciously led by the Holy Spirit in our acts of worship. There are times he wants us to shout of his greatness; other times to bow low before him in quiet reverence. Remember, it is not so much how we want to express it, but rather how God wants to receive it!

A Lighthouse of Worship

One of the best ways to prepare for lighthouse ministry is to worship God, and the best way to prepare to worship him is to reflect on the wonder of the Lord. Messenger Fellowship offers two resources for helping you establish your lighthouse as a lighthouse of worship:

- My book, *A God Who Heals the Heart,* a forty-day devotional, takes the reader on a journey toward knowing God intimately, helping the reader to rekindle his or her passion for him. This book is an excellent resource for personal or group Bible studies or to share with unbelievers who have tough questions about God.

▸ "Thy Kingdom Come," a musical CD and prayer guide. For those who have a passion for revival in this country, this musical presents some vital keys to preparing for a national awakening. Complete with prayer guide, this resource is an excellent intercession tool for prayer teams, small groups, and churches.

To order, call or write:

Steve Fry Ministries
Box 474
Brentwood, TN 37024
615-370-1322
sfmin@compuserve.com

Integrity Music offers several CDs and videos that I recommend and that can be used for small group worship as you prepare your heart to light up your neighborhood for Christ. Among them are:

▸ Celebrate Jesus 2000, the official recording of Mission America's CJ2000 evangelistic outreach.

▸ B.C./A.D. SPLIT TIME, an evangelistic CD to be used in your personal witnessing outreach.

▸ World's Best Praise & Worship, a collection of the world's best praise and worship songs that is over an hour in length.

To order Celebrate Jesus 2000 resource materials from Integrity Direct please call toll-free at 1-800-533-6912. For all Internet orders: www.integritymusic.com. Also available wherever Christian Music is sold.

***Steven Fry is the producer and director of the Storyteller Project, a resource to get the teaching Jesus into the hands of millions of people, and author of the book* A God Who Heals the Heart.**

Thirty-Three

Lighthouses for Disabled People

—Marlys Taege—

"Come to me, all you who are weary and burdened, and I will give you rest."

Matthew 11:28

There's something about our fallen natures that makes us fear—even to the point of avoiding—people or situations we're not used to. People often avoid contact with individuals with disabilities out of that kind of fear. They know little or nothing about disabilities, and they may not even know a disabled person, so they're afraid of saying something wrong, afraid of the discomfort they may feel at having to face someone who is disabled, afraid of the guilt they may feel over that discomfort.

So, rather than face that kind of discomfort, most people choose to avoid those who are disabled.

People with disabilities represent an oft-neglected yet vast mission field. As we work to establish our lighthouses, we need to be ready should a person with a disability cross our paths. And, with more than fifty million disabled people living in the United States alone, it is only a matter of time before we meet one of these valuable people.

We need to keep in mind that God values the disabled person as much as he values the "able-bodied," that Jesus died for those with disabilities and that he has given each of them talents and gifts that are to be used to glorify him.

When you meet a disabled person—be it someone who is vision or hearing impaired, someone who is in a wheelchair, or someone with any sort of physical or mental disability—keep in mind that apart from their disability, they are like anyone else: They want understanding and not pity, friendship and not fear. And, just like anyone else, they need Jesus Christ.

Don't be afraid to greet a disabled person the same way you would anyone else. If there is one thing I hear almost universally from the disabled people I know, it is that they wish people would just relax and treat them the way they treat other people they meet.

Feel the freedom to offer a disabled person a hand of friendship, or to strike up a conversation the way you would with anyone else. Most of all, don't be afraid to show them—through your words and your deeds—the love that Jesus has offered them.

Show the disabled man or woman the kind of respect you would anyone else. Offer your assistance, but don't force it on that person. Speak to him or her naturally, not with a tone of pity or discomfort. And, of course, feel free to invite them to participate in church and social events that could expose them to the gospel of Christ.

There are many places to find assistance in learning how to minister to disabled people. Here is a list of ministries for disabled people and for those wishing to be enabled to minister to disabled people:

Blindness and Vision Impairments:

CARE Ministries, Inc.
P.O. Box 1830
Starkville, MN 39760
1-800-336-2232
www.careministries.org

Chronic Pain:
And He Will Give You Rest
P.O. Box 502886
San Diego, CA 92150
619-237-1698
www.ixpres.com/jlcopen
E-mail: rest@ixpres.com

Deafness and Hearing Impairments:
Deaf Missions
21199 Greenview Rd.
Council Bluffs, IA 51503-9500
712-322-5493 (V/TTY)

Developmental Disabilities:
National Christian Resource Center
700 Hoffmann Dr.
Watertown, WI 53094
1-800-369-INFO (4636)

Environmental Illness:
(allergies, chronic fatigue syndrome, and fibromyalgia)
Share, Care and Prayer
P.O. Box 2080
Frazier Park, CA 93225
www.sharecareprayer.org
Fax: 661-245-6614
E-mail: janetfp@juno.com
(They will mail you a resource packet.)

Mental Illness:
Pathways to Promise
5400 Arsenal St.
St. Louis, MO 63139
314-644-8400

Physical Disabilities:
JAF Ministries
P.O. Box 3333
Agoura Hills, CA 91301
818-707-5664
www.jafministries.com

The Christian Council on Persons with Disabilities is a partnership of ministries that focus on a variety of Christian outreaches to persons with disabilities. If you want to know more about CCPD or would like to start a local chapter, contact Marlys Taege, 7120 W. Dove Court, Milwaukee, WI 53223, marlys@execpc.com or phone 414-357-6672 (phone and fax).

Marlys Taege is executive director of Christian Council on Persons with Disabilities.

Thirty-Four

Trained Lighthouse Keepers

—DR. DOUGLAS SHAW—

Always be prepared to give an answer to everyone who asks you to give the reason for the hope that you have.

1 PETER 3:15

My religious roots are from India and include a Muslim great-grandfather and a Yogi grandfather, both of whom found Jesus Christ as the way, the truth, and the life.

Despite all the dramatic changes that take place in our world literally on a daily basis, one thing has remained and will always remain the same: the gospel message. It is the same message that Jesus preached two thousand years ago and the same message that reached the heart of my great-grandfather and grandfather years ago. It is the same message I've had the privilege of preaching here in the United States and of taking overseas for more than twenty-five years. It is the same message we need to preach today.

The more than 100 million people in the U.S. with little or no comprehension or connection with the light and the love of the Lord Jesus Christ present a unique challenge, but a challenge God can equip us to meet.

The Sharing Jesus Training Manual in its user-friendly format includes interactive learning, which will help take the fear out of witnessing. It is designed to educate and inspire a Christian to an effective personalized action plan. Taken individually or in a group, the course provides the following:

▸ **A clear concise presentation of the message.** The uniqueness of Jesus Christ and what he offers is presented within the context of world religions. It presents Jesus as who he is: Savior and Lord without equal or parallel.

▸ **A clear concise understanding of the Messenger.** The teaching 1) focuses on why we do not witness effectively, and 2) empowers students to reactivate a personal passion for the spiritually lost.

▸ **A clear concise understanding of the mission.** Using the examples of Jesus, Paul, and other models, the course shows how to dialogue with people through friendship evangelism. It seeks to eliminate feelings of intimidation that come from not being a scholar or expert by presenting easily understandable charts on what people believe. With the use of role–playing, a personalized witnessing style is developed, resulting in a new sense of confidence.

You will find Sharing Jesus is a cutting edge evangelism resource for personal witnessing in the new millennium. For more information on Sharing Jesus seminars and how you can order manuals for your church or denomination, please write: Douglas Shaw, Seminars/Ministry Resources, P.O. Box 276384, Sacramento, CA 95827. Phone: 916-362-8401, Fax: 916-362-3625.

Dr. Douglas Shaw of Sharing Jesus Seminars has served as a director of the Beyond '99 evangelism initiative as well as the Mission America Committee.

Thirty-Five

When a Neighbor Comes to Christ

—STEVE DOUGLASS—

For you know that we dealt with each of you as a father deals with his own children, encouraging, comforting and urging you to live lives worthy of God, who calls you into his kingdom and glory.

1 THESSALONIANS 1:11–12

Suppose that as a result of your role as a lighthouse keeper, some of your neighbors come to Christ. You have prayed they would. You expressed Christ's love and shared his message with them so that they would. Now that they have, what next? What is your responsibility to them?

New Christians need a lot of help getting established in their faith, and you are likely the nearest source of that help and possibly the one they are most willing to respond to initially. For that reason, you need to follow up. You need to provide encouragement and guidance to those you have led to Christ.

Follow Up Immediately

Three of the most common reasons people initially fall away from faith in Christ are doubt and confusion, continued sin, and pressure from friends. You must recognize these potential problems and help people avoid them. Here are some guidelines for doing that:

1. New Christians need answers about their doubts and confusion.

You need to provide them with assurance of their salvation. Three passages of Scripture you may use are Revelation 3:20, John 5:11–13, and Hebrews 13:5b. These passages focus on what God has done and will do for them: come into their lives, give them eternal life, and never forsake them.

2. New Christians need encouragement in not continuing in their sin. You need to show them how to appropriate God's power to resist sin and live out the righteousness God desires. Ephesians 3:16 and 5:18 point to the role of God's Holy Spirit as the internal strength and power to live the Christian life. Since people are likely to continue to sin some, you need to explain their need to confess their sins and turn from them (1 John 1:8–9).

3. New Christians need encouragement in resisting pressure from friends. This problem is tricky. It may be difficult to persuade new Christians to abandon longstanding friendships with non-Christians that are pulling them down spiritually. The single best thing you can do is to become more of a friend to them yourself. Encounter them daily if possible. Be especially sensitive to their needs. Increasingly take the role of a guide in this new and important step they have taken.

Help Establish Them

It isn't enough to do the immediate follow-up then just leave the new convert alone. You need to help establish new Christians further in three critical areas:

1. Understanding. The Christian life is new to those who are new to the faith, and they don't know the basics of how to live it. They don't know, for example, about the importance of daily Bible study and prayer, and even if they do, they don't know how to do these things effectively.

One of the best things you can do for new believers is point them to a Bible study for new Christians available near them. It may be in your neighborhood, or at least on your end of town. It may be in a home or in a church. Be careful to place the new Christians in studies taught by people who live out the Christian life, not just talk about it.

2. A relationship with God. With all the input the new Christians may receive from you and others, it might be easy to miss a very fundamental point: the Christian faith is all about fellowship with God. The Lord created Adam and Eve to have fellowship with him. In heaven, we will have eternal fellowship with God. In between those two ends of time, the Bible is all about restoring and maintaining close fellowship with God (see 1 John 1). You need to help new Christians cultivate a "personalness" (intimacy) with God through prayer, reading the Scripture, and in other ways.

3. Relationships with other Christians. People are greatly influenced by their friends. When people come to Christ, especially out of sinful lifestyles, they may have a lot of friends who will continue to influence them toward sin and away from Christian growth.

The best antidote to that is displacement. You need to guide new Christians toward formation of new friendships with vital Christians. As new Christian friendships exert influence toward Christ, the influence of the old friendships will be displaced (diminished). There are several places this can happen, including in their neighborhoods and in churches (for example, in Sunday school classes).

Wherever they begin to attend to learn about Christian growth, they need to be encouraged and affirmed in forming new friendships. For many people, new relationships are crucially important. For that reason, you need to lead the new Christians to attend, and eventually join, a good church.

Help!

Perhaps you feel over your head as you contemplate doing all of these things. Join the club! Most believers would not be naturally excellent at everything that is needed to provide follow-up for new Christians.

So, what can you do? Two things:

1. Involve others. Ask your pastor, Bible class teacher, or other mature Christians if they could help with the follow-up process, or if they could recommend others who could help.

2. Use follow-up materials. There are excellent Bible studies, videos, audiotapes, and other materials offered by many denominations and parachurch organizations to help you with your follow-up. You may also want to ask some of your mature Christian friends what materials they find most helpful in following up new Christians.

Although following up may be challenging to you, it will make a tremendous difference in the lives of new believers around you.

Steve Douglass is executive vice president of Campus Crusade For Christ.

Mission America Committee Directory

Honorary Co-Chairmen

Dr. Bill Bright
Rev. Billy Graham
Dr. John Perkins

Honorary Advisory Committee

Rev. Reinhard Bonnke, Christ For All Nations
Mrs. Vonette Bright, Women Today International
Dr. D. Stuart Briscoe, Elmbrook Church
Dr. Luis Bush, AD2000 and Beyond Movement
Mr. Charles Colson, Prison Fellowship
Dr. Loren Cunningham, Youth with a Mission International
Dr. Martin DeHaan, RBC Ministries
Dr. James Dobson, Focus an the Family
Mrs. Shirley Dobson, Focus on the Family
Dr. Ted W. Engstrom, World Vision
Dr. Leighton Ford and Dr. Millard Fuller, Habitat for Humanity
Rev. John Guest, John Guest Evangelistic Team
Dr. Jack Hayford, Church On The Way
Dr. James B. Henry, First Baptist Church Orlando
Dr. Sterling W. Huston, Billy Graham Evangelistic Association
Rev. Max Lucado, Oak Hills Church of Christ
Dr. John C. Maxwell, INJOY
Mr. Bill McCartney, Promise Keepers
Dr. James Montgomery, Dawn Ministries
Mr. Harold L. Myra, Christianity Today
Ms. Dellanna O'Brien, Women's Missionary Union
Dr. Lloyd John Ogilvie, U.S. Senate—Chaplain
Dr. Luis Palau, Luis Palau Evangelistic Association
Dr. Pat Robertson, Christian Broadcasting Network, Inc.
Dr. Adrian Rogers, Belvue Baptist Church
Dr. Robert Schuller, Crystal Cathedral
Dr. Robert A. Seiple, U.S. State Department
Mr. Richard E. Stearns, World Vision
Dr. Ravi Zacharias, Ravi Zacharias International Ministries

Facilitation Committee

Dr. Paul Cedar, Chair, Mission America
Bishop George McKinney, V-Chair, St. Stephen's Church
Dr. Lonnie Allison, Secretary, Billy Graham Center
Dr. Roger Parrott, Treasurer, Belhaven College
Dr. Don Argue, Northwest College
Dr. David Bryant, Concerts of Prayer International
Mrs. Bobbye Byerly, World Prayer Center
Bishop Rorlerick Caesar, Bethel Gospel Tabernacle Fellowship
Rev. Patricia Chen, First Love Ministries International
Dr. Robert E. Coleman, Trinity Evangelical Divinity School
Dr. Stephen B. Douglass, Campus Crusade for Christ
Dr. Tom Fortson, Promise Keepers
Dr. H. Eddie Fox, World Evang. World Methodist Council
Rev. Dave Gibson, Mission America
Ms. Mary Glazier, Wind Walkers International
Dr. Larry L. Lewis, Mission America
Bishop Nathaniel Linsey, Christian Methodist Episcopal Church
Rev. Paul McKaughan, Evan. Fellowship of Mission Agencies
Dr. Jesse Miranda, AMEN
Dr. Tom Phillips, International Students Inc.
Mrs. Mary Lance Sisk, Love Your Neighbor Ministries
Dr. Thomas Trask, Assemblies of God
Dr. Lamar Vest, National Association of Evangelicals
Dr. Thomas Wang, Great Commission International
Rev. Rick Warren, Saddleback Community Church

General Committee

Dr. Joe Aldrich, International Renewal Ministries
Dr. Dallas Anderson, Evangelical Covenant Church
Dr. Neil Anderson, Freedom in Christ Ministries
Mr. Mark Anderson, Youth With a Mission
Mr. Alan Andrews, U.S. Navigators
Dr. Bob Andringa, Coalition of Christian Colleges and Universities
Dr. Thomas E. Armiger, International Center of the Wesleyan Church
Mrs. Kay Arthur, Precept Ministries
Mr. Arthur J. Athens, Officers' Christian Fellowship
Dr. Theodore Baehr, The Christian Film & TV Commission
Ms. Tryna Bahl, Lydia Fellowship International
Dr. Dennis Baker, NexStep-SWBC
Dr. Robert Bakke, Evangelical Free Church of America
Ms. Winnie Bartel, World Evangelical Fellowship
Rev. Glenn A. Barth, Mission America
Dr. Allan H. Beeber, Campus Crusade for Christ International
Dr. V. Gilbert Beers, Scripture Press Ministries
Rev. Russell Begaye, Multiethnic Church Plating NAMB
Dr. B. Clayton Bell Sr., Highland Park Presbyterian Church
Mr. Gary P. Bergel, Intercessors for America
Dr. Henry T. Blackaby, North American Mission Board SBC
Mr. Dennis Blevins, Mission Portland
Mr. Ron Boehme, YWAM/Renewal Ministries
Dr. Jim L. Bond, Church of the Nazarene/International Headquarters
Dr. Corinthia Boone, Together in Ministry International
Dr. Peter Borgdorff, Christian Reformed Church of North America
Mr. Ed Boschman, MISSION USA
Dr. Everett R. Boyce, Association of Christians Ministering to Internationals
Mrs. Mary Ann Bridgewater, Promise Reapers
Mr. Norman Brinkley, Inland Empire 2000 & Beyond
Mrs. Catherine Brokke, Bethany Fellowship Missions
Mr. Gene Brooks, Mission Carolina
Dr. George K. Brushaber, Bethel College and Seminary
Dr. Clifton E. Buckrham Sr., Habitat for Humanity
Mr. Patrick Burke, Mr. Doug Burleigh, Russian Ministries
Dr. Phill Butler, Interdev
Rev. David Butts, Harvest Prayer Ministries
Mr. Randy L. Carlson, Family Life Communications, Inc.
Mr. Fred Carpenter, Mars Hill Productions
Dr. Harold Carter, New Shiloh Baptist Church
Mr. Brian Chandler, Be the LIGHT Ministries, Inc.
Dr. Charles Chaney, Rev. Jean-Claude Chevalme, Love in the Name of Christ
Rev. Clifford Christensen, Conservative Cong. Christian Conference
Mrs. Evelyn Christenson, United Prayer Ministry
Mr. Huron Claus, CHIEF, Inc.
Mr. Tom Claus, CHIEF, Inc.
Mr. Bonn Clayton, The Renewal Fellowship
Mr. Chris Cooper, Mapping Center for Evangelism
Dr. Charles Crabtree, Assemblies of God
Dr. Roger Cross, Youth for Christ/USA
Mr. King A. Crow, Faith Works
Mr. Bob Cryder, Bob Cryder Team Ministries
Dr. Bob Culver, InterFACE Ministries
Rev. Timothy Dahlin, John Guest Evangelistic Team
Mr. John B. Damoose, Freedom Ministries of America
Mrs. Carol Davis, Global Spectrum—The Urban Group
Dr. L. Edward Davis, Evangelical Presbyterian Church
Mr. Everett Davis, Jesus Video Project/CCC
Rev. John Dawson, International Reconciliation Coalition
Dr. Jack Dennison, Dawn Ministries
Mr. Drew Dickens, Mission America/NEED HIM Project
Rev. Terry Dirks, Intl. Renewal Ministries
Mr. George Dooms, Team Impact
Dr. Lewis A. Drummond, Beeson Divinity School/Samford University
Dr. Wesley Duewel, OMS International Inc.
Dr. Maxie D. Dunnam, Asbury Theological Seminary
Dr. Dick Eastman, Every Home for Christ
Rev. Elward Ellis, Crossroads Presbyterian Church
Dr. Gordon A. England, Promise Keepers
Mrs. Gretchen Englund, Christian Women's Network
Mr. Paul Eshleman, The JESUS Film Project
Dr. Louis Evans, Menlo Park Presbyterian Church
Mrs. Colleen Evans, Menlo Park Presbyterian Church
Rev. Jeff Farmer, Open Bible Churches
Dr. Richard Allen Farmer, RAF Ministries Inc.
Mr. Bill Fay, Hope Ministries
Mr. Tom Felten, Sports Spectrum Magazine
Dr. Robert E. Fisher, Center for Ministerial Care
Rev. Paul Fleischmann, National Network of Youth Ministries
Dr. Edward L. Foggs, Church of God
Mr. G. P. Foote III, CCC/International Student Resources
Dr. Paul Ford, Church Resource Ministries
Rev. Francis Frangipane, Advancing Church Ministries
Rev. K. Gerone Free, Greater Mt. Carmel Baptist Church
Mr. Greg Fritz, Caleb Project
Mrs. Naomi Frizzell, Mission America
Rev. Joseph L. Garlington, Covenant Church of Pittsburgh
Rev. Dennis Gaylor, Chi Alpha Campus Ministries
Dr. Timothy George, Beeson Divinity School
Rev. Armin Gesswein, Revival Prayer Fellowship, Inc.
Ms. Joyce Godwin, International Students, Inc.
Rev. LaRue Goetz, STEER, Inc.
Dr Stephen Goold, Crystal Evangelical Free Church
Mr. Dennis L. Gorton, Christian and Missionary Alliance
Mr. Jonathan Graf, Pray! Magazine
Ms. Kathryn S. Grant, AD2000 Women's Track
Mrs. Mary Greenhalge, Fragrance of Love, Inc.
Mrs. Carol Guess, Mission Virginia
Dr. E. Brandt Gustavson, National Religious Broadcasters
Dr. Cornell Haan, Mission America
Dr. Eugene Habecker, American Bible Society
Rev. Charles Hackett, General Council of Assemblies of God
Rev. Norval Hadley, Evangelical Friends Mission
Rev. Ted Haggard, New Life Church
Dr. William Hamel, Evangelical Free Church of America
Dr. Alistair Hanna, Alpha North America
Ms. Jane Hansen, Aglow International
Dr. David C. Hansley, Home Missions and Evangelism OFWB
Rev. Charles Hanson, Congregational Holiness Church, Inc.
Mr. Kevin Harlan, Fellowship of Christian Athletes
Dr. Richard H. Harris, North American Mission Board SBC
Dr. John A. Hash, Bible Pathways
Mr. Steve Hawthorne, WayMakers
Dr. Stephen A. Hayner, InterVarsity Christian Fellowship
Dr. Michael Haynes, Twelfth Baptist Church
Mr. James V. Heidinger II, Good News Movement
Mr. Jaan Heinmets, THE NET—Serving Together
Dr. David W. Henderson, Covenant Presbyterian Church
Mr. J. Scott Hesler, Chinese Christian Church of Washington, D.C.

Mr. Fred Heumann, Music Works International
Ms. Catherine Hickem, Center Peace Ministries
Mr. David Hicks, Operation Mobilization
Rev. Greg Hicks, Mission Portland
Dr. C. B. Hogue, Southern Baptist Convention
Dr. Stephen Hoke, Church Resource Ministries
Mr. Bruce Hubby, Professional Dynametric Progs, Inc.
Dr. John A. Huffman Jr., St. Andrews Presbyterian Church
Rev. Clyde M. Hughes, International Pentecostal Church of Christ
Dr. R. Kent Hughes, College Church in Wheaton
Rev. Bill Hull, Evangelical Free Church of Cypress
Rev. Todd Hunter, Association of Vineyard Churches
Rev. Ron Hutchcraft, Ron Hutchcraft Ministries, Inc.
Rev. Jim Hylton, MetroChurch
Mr. Peter Iliyn, Youth With a Mission
Mrs. Esther S. Ilnisky, Esther Network International
Mrs. Cindy Jacobs, General of Intercession
Mr. Mike Jacobs, General of Intercession
Mr. Timothy James, Truth International Ministries
Mr. Stan Jeter, CBN News
Dr. Raimundo Jimenez, Hispanic Christian Community Network
Rev. Gerry Johnson, SIM Ethnic Focus Ministry
Rev. Calvin Johnson, Solid Rock Christian Church
Dr. Ezra Earl Jones, United Methodist Board of Discipleship
Mr. Brad Jurkovich, By His LIGHT Ministries, Inc.
Dr. John C. K. Kim, University of California Monterey
Dr. Dennis Kinlaw, Francis Asbury Society
Dr. Jerry Kirk, Coalition Against Pornography
Mr. Chuck Klein, CCC/Student Venture
Bishop Richard Kohl, Evangelical Congregational Church
Rev. Jerry M Kosberg, Lutheran Church/Missouri Synod
Dr. John E. Kyle, Evangelical Fellowship of Mission Agencies
Lt. Ralph Labbee, The Salvation Army
Mr. Joe Lachnit, Rev. J. Paul Landrey, Christ for the City International
Rev. T. A. Lanes, Assemblies of God International Fellowship
Dr. Paul Larsen, Evangelical Covenant Church
Mr. Kenneth R. Larson, Slumberland, Inc.
Rev. James D. Leggett, International Pentecostal Holiness Church
Mr. Michael Lienau, Global Net Productions
Dr. Duane Litfin, Wheaton College
Dr. Michael Little, The Christian Broadcasting Network
Rev. H.B. London Jr., Focus on the Family
Rev. Don Long, International Church of Foursquare Gospel
Rev. Lowell Lundstrom, Lowell Lundstrom Ministries
Ms. Lorry Lutz, AD2000 Women's Track
Dr. Erwin Lutzer, The Moody Church
Rev. Stephen Macchia, Vision New England
Ms. Carol Madison, Bloomington Evangelical Free Church
Rev. David Mains, Chapel of the Air
Dr. Osvaldo O. Marino, Doxa International University
Mr. Jeff Marks, New England Concerts of Prayer
Mrs. Mary Marr, Widow's Mite Foundation
Dr. James Earl Massey, Dr. John Mathison, Frazer Memorial United Methodist Church
Rev. Winston Mattson-Boze, Assemblies of God Intl. Fellowship
Rev. Michael J. McCaskey, The Pocket Testament League
Ms. Janet McGee, Aglow International
Rev. Roy B. McKeown, World Opportunities International
Rev. Wm. Dwight McKissic Sr., Cornerstone Baptist Church
Mr. Bruce McNicol, Leadership Catalyst Inc.
Ms. Bernita Melancon, Aglow International
Mr. Marty Melwin, International Reconciliation Coalition
Rev. Phil Miglioratti, National Pastor's Prayer Network
Mr. Mark Mittelberg, Willow Creek Association
Mr. Patrick M. Morley, Man in the Mirror
Dr. Jim Mulkey, Hope for a Generation
Mrs. Andrea Mullins, Women's Missionary Union
Dr. Bryant Myers, Ward Vision
Rev Charles Mylander, Friends Church Southwest
Mr. James M. Neal, Dad the Family Shepherd
Mr. Grant Nelson, The Nelson Family Foundation
Mr. Robert W. Norsworthy, International Students, Inc.
Mr. Lloyd Olson, Jesus Video Project/CCC
Rev. Karl Overbeek, Church of the Chimes
Rev. Robert M. Overgaard Sr., Church of the Lutheran Brethren
Mrs. Carol Owens, Heal Our Land
Rev. Jimmy Owens, Heal Our Land
Mr. Kevin Palau, Luis Palau Evangelistic Association
Rev. John Palmer, First Assembly of God
Mr. Greg Parsons, U.S. Center for World Mission
Dr. Ben Patterson, Hope College
Dr. Virginia Patterson, Children's Ministries of America
Mr. John Pearson, Christian Management Association
Rev. Wayne Pederson, Northwestern College and Radio
Mr. Tom Pelton, March for Jesus
Dr. Keith Phillips, Ward Impact, Inc.
Rev. Randy Phillips, Promise Keepers
Rev. Earl Pickard, PrayerWorks
Rev. Mac Pier, Concerts of Prayer Greater New York
Mr. Larry Pierce, Religion News Today
Dr. Lyle Pointer, Church of the Nazarene
Rev. Mark Pollard, The Common Ground Movement
Rev. Randy Pope, Perimeter Church
Rev. John Quam, Mission America
Dr. David Rambo, Alliance Theological Seminary
Mr. Paul Ramseyer, Northwestern College & Radio
Dr. W. Duncan Rankin, Reformed Seminary
Mr. Robert Rasmussen, International Messengers
Dr. Robert Reccord, North American Mission Board SBC
Rev. Brent Regis, Christ for All Nations
Dr. Dwight Reighard, North Star Church
Bishop Jose A. Reyes Sr., Church of God of Prophecy
Dr. Robert S. Ricker, Baptist General Conference
Dr. Stacy Rinehart, The Navigators
Dr. Darrell W. Robinson, Total Church Life Min., Inc./NAMB
Rev. Moises Rodriquez, North American Mission Board
Mr. Dave Roever, Roever Evangelistic Association
Rev. Randall Roth, First Covenant Church
Rev. Steve Russo, Steve Russo Evangelistic Team
Mr. Dennis Rydberg, Young Life
Mr. Michael C. Sack, Cultural Insights, Inc.
Mr. Hal H. Sacks, BridgeBuilders International, Inc.
Rev. Harold Salem, First Baptist Church
Rev. Jim Schaedler, Utah Games Network
Rev. Dale Schlafer, Rev. Bobby Sena, North American Mission Board
Dr. Doug Shaw, Christ for All Nations
Dr. Dal Shealy, Fellowship of Christian Athletes
Mr. Glenn Sheppard, International Prayer Ministries
Dr. David Shibley, Global Advance
Mr. Clarence Shuler, Focus on the Family
Rev. Charles R. Shumate, Church of God
Rev. Harvey Sider, The Moderator
Rev. Edgardo Silvoso, Harvest Evangelism, Inc.
Rev. Jerome Simpson, International Bible Society
Pastor J. D. Smith, East Gate/IMPACT
Mr. Terrell Smith, InterVarsity Christian Fellowship
Mr. Rolland Smith, Mission Omega
Rev. Eddie Smith, U.S. Prayer Track
Bishop Chet Smith, Congregational Holiness Church
Mr. Reilly R. Smith, The Brethren Church
Mr. Dan Southern, American Tract Society
Dr. Dann Spader, SONLIFE Ministries
Mr. Barry St. Clair, Reachout Ministries
Rev. Darryl Starnes, African Methodist Episcopal Zion Church
Rev. Tom Stebbins, Evangelism Explosion III International
Dr. Stephen Steele, Dawn Ministries
Rev. Jean Steffenson, Intl. Reconciliation Coalition
Rev. Paul Strand, Bethany Fellowship International
Dr. Bill Sullivan, Church of the Nazarene/International Headquarters
Dr. Vinson Synan, Regent University School of Divinity
Mrs. Joni Eareckson Tada, JAF Ministries
Mr. John Tayloe, High Adventure
Dr. Terry Taylor, The Navigators
Mrs. Chizuyo Templeman, Japanese Southern Baptist Church of America
Dr. Terry Teykl, Renewal Ministries
Pastor Ron Thaxton, Celebrate Jesus West Virginia
Mr. David F. Thornton, USC/Thornton Foundation
Rev. Sammy Tippit, God's Love in Action
Ms. Becky Tirabassi, Change Your Life
Dr. Joseph Tkach, Worldwide Church of God
Dr. Elmer Towns, Liberty University
Mr. Johnny Travis, Breath of Life Worship Center
Mr. Wesley Tullis, Youth With a Mission
Dr. Forrest Turpen, Christian Educators Association International
Rev. Richard L. Twiss, Wiconi International
Bishop Kenneth Ulmer, Faithful Center Missionary Baptist Church
Lt. Colonel Richard Ulyat, The Salvation Army
Dr. Alvin J. Vander Griend, Mission 21 HOPE
Dr. C. Peter Wagner, AD2000 United Prayer Track
Rev. Bill Waldrop, Mission America
Rev. Jarvis Ward, Mission America
Com. Robert A. Watson, The Salvation Army
Mr. Eddie Waxer, International Sports Coalition
Mr. Bob Waymire, Light International
Mr. Dolphus Weary, Mission Mississippi
Mr. Bob Weiner, Bob Weiner Ministries
Dr. Daniel Weiss, American Baptist Churches in the USA
Mr. Thomas White, Frontline Ministries
Dr. Luder Whitlock Jr., Reformed Theological Seminary
Dr. Bruce Wilkinson, Walk through the Bible/CoMission
Dr. Georgalyn Wilkinson, Gospel Literature International
Bishop Oswill Williams, Church of God of Prophecy
Dr. Lorraine Williams, Pittsburgh Leadership Foundation
Dr. John P. Williams Jr., Evangelical Friends Church
Dr. Jim Wilson, Jim Wilson Evangelistic Association
Rev. Tim Wilson, Mission America
Mr. Steve Wingfield, Steve Wingield Ministries
Dr. Ralph Winter, U.S. Center for World Missions
Mr. Mike Woodruff, The Ivy Jungle Network
Mr. Dennis Worden, EQUIP
Dr. Richard Wynn, Emerging Young Leaders
Dr. Ted Yamamori, Food for the Hungry
Dr. John O. Yarbrough, North American Mission Board/SBC
Rev. Wayne Yarnall, Primitive Methodist Church
Mr. Jerry Yellowhawk, Wesleyan Native American Ministries

Mission America

5666 Lincoln Drive, Suite100
Edina, MN 55436
Phone:(612)912-0001
Fax: (612)912-0002
E-mail: missionamerica@Compuserve.com
Internet: www.missionamerica.org

Celebrate Jesus 2000

RESOURCE GUIDE

Prayer

Personal Evangelism Praying

Lighthouse of Prayer Brochure
A must-have for every CJ2000 participant. This brochure details a vital strategy bringing believers together in small groups to pray.

Bringing My World to Christ
This simple Evangelism-Prayer ministry is used in praying for lost people and the salvation of their souls.

Love Your Neighbor as Yourself
A practical way to pray for and love your neighbors to Christ.

Praying Your Friends to Christ
A small pamphlet designed to assist Christians in praying for lost people.

Evangelism Prayer Cells

Make Your Home a Power House Alvin Vander Griend
Discover how prayer can powerfully change your life and your neighborhood.

PrayerWalking
Everything you need to organize prayerwalking through a zip code, or an entire community.

Reach 3
An exciting plan for men to reach three other men with the gospel.

A Time to Pray God's Way Evelyn Christenson
A simple plan to help you have the greatest influence on your world.

City-Wide & National Prayer Movements

PrayUSA!
A coalition of denominations and Christian organizations encouraging 40 days of prayer each year prior to Easter. Resources present specific themes each year. PrayUSA! '99 will be from February 17 to March 28. Theme: "Seek God for the City."

Creative Approaches for Concerts of Prayer David Bryant
Discover dynamic new ways to format balanced strategic praying in a Concert of Prayer.

Fasting & Prayer
Fasting and Prayer national event held each year in November. Thosands of satellite locations around the United States.

Heal Our Land
A musical prayer event which enables church leadership to rally an army of prayer intercessors to meet God's conditions for the healing of our land.

Prayer Summits
A four day, nondenominational worship and prayer conference for church leadership.

Other

Prayer the Great Adventure Dr. David Jeremiah
Dr. Jeremiah shares his heart—both blessings and struggles—to provide insights that teach us how to embark on the most satisfying of trips, the great adventure of prayer.

When Mother's Pray Cheri Fuller
This book offers encouragement and a larger perspective to women, presenting compelling insights about what God can do in the lives of our children when we pray.

31 Days of Prayer Ruth Myers
The book guides believers through prayer for thirty-one days, allowing for personalized prayer that reflects individual circumstances and areas for spiritual growth.

7 Basic Steps to Successful Fasting & Prayer Bill Bright
This handy reference guide provides simple steps for beginning and ending your fast and suggests a practical plan for prayer and a daily nutritional schedule.

Pray! Magazine NavPress
Pray! is a prayer tool created specifically for people who are serious about prayer. If you want to unleash the awesome power of prayer in your Christian walk, *Pray!* will stir the coals of your prayer life and keep them burning.

More Resources

Experiencing God Henry Blackaby
Learn to hear when God is speaking to you. Find out where God is working and join him. Experience God doing through you what only God can do!

The Hour That Changes the World Dick Eastman
Provides a unique, time-tested, 12-step prayer strategy that has revitalized the prayer lives of thousands of Christians.

House of Prayer
This video series shows how your church can launch an effective House of Prayer ministry in the neighborhoods and workplaces of Christians.

Local Church Evangelism-Prayer Guide
Teaches the necessity of evangelism-praying and provides guidelines for local churches wishing to saturate the church with evangelism-prayer.

Prayer Pacesetters Sourcebook:
How to Start and Nurture a Community Prayer Movement David Bryant
Describes the way in which God has been giving a unity of vision and practical implementational approaches across a diverse set of localities.

Prayor'tize Phil Mighoratti
Resources for pastors and churches that have made prayer a priority.

Reunitus Joe Aldrich
Building bridges to each other through prayer summits.

The Transforming Power of Fasting & Prayer Bill Bright
God is moving through His church in a deep and powerful way, through fasting and prayer, to bring His people closer to Him. Includes stirring accounts of Christians who have been part of the fasting and prayer movement that is erupting across the country.

U.S. Prayer Directory
Comprehensive list of ministries dedicated to encouraging churches to pray.

Christian Educators Association International
Various resources available to use in praying for your schools and teachers.

Personal Witness

Training Materials

Becoming a Contagious Christian Bill Hybels & Mark Mittelberg
Learn to communicate your faith in a style that fits you.

The Case for Christ Lee Strobel
Learn an intellectual defense of your faith as a former journalist and atheist traces his quest for the case for Christ.

People Sharing Jesus Darrell W. Robinson
This evangelism course teaches how to communicate the gospel easily, naturally, and joyfully.

Christian Life and Witness Video Course
Learn how to put faith into action and effectively witness and field questions from nonbelievers.

Evangelism Explosion
Variety of training resources, books, videos, etc. for effective personal evangelism.

Gospel Literature

Beyond '99/From Minus to Plus Reinhard Bonnke
Learn more about this booklet that will be sent to potentially 125 million homes in the United States and Canada in 1999, sharing the saving message of Jesus Christ.

Beyond '99 New Testament
Contemporary English Version New Testament with "Understanding and Experiencing the New Life" and "The Spiritual Journal."

CJ2000 New Testament
Includes Billy Graham's *Steps to Peace with God* and "Romans Road" evangelism notes.

Discovery NIV New Testament

The single-column softcover New Testament is excellent for introducing your neighbors or coworkers to the word of God. Includes a "journal narrative" that explores key questions and how the Bible answers them.

The Journey Bible

This NIV Bible is designed to draw seekers and new believers into God's Word through practical illustrations that deal with major life issues.

Tracts

Mission America Church Variety Pack

Samples of tracts churches and individuals can use to engage people in talking about a personal relationship with Christ.

Split Time Tract

This evangleistic pocket-guide will be a foundational witnessing piece used during Celebrate Jesus 2000

Billy Graham: Steps to Peace with God

An effective, nonthreatening way to pass along the Lord's life-saving message

Have You Heard of the Four Spiritual Laws? Campus Crusade for Christ

This booklet explains the four spiritual laws and what must be done to receive Christ as Savior.

It's Awesome

This booklet shares the Good News, how Jesus is God's provision for salvation from sin, and how we can receive the gift of salvation.

Yours for Life! Ron Hutchcraft

In this minibooklet, the core Gospel message of Jesus Christ is presented in easy-to-understand language. An ideal contemporary witnessing tool for all ages.

Videos

The Harvest

A crisis at harvest. A family pushed to the edge. A young boy's prayer echoing through heaven. Inspired by a true story.

Jesus Video

This film takes you back 2000 years to the life of Jesus Christ and is taken directly from the Gospel of Luke.

More Resources

Lifestyle Evangelism Joe Aldrich

Dr. Joe Aldrich shows us how we can build genuine, caring relationships with nonbelievers that will open their hearts to the gospel message.

The Gift for all People Max Lucado

This book provides Christians with a unique, warm, and attractive presentation of the gospel to give to non-Christian family or friends.

Absolutely Sure Steven Lawson

People must be awakened out of their slumber and shown the evidences of a true work of grace in salvation. The greatest proof of the new birth is not a past event, but a present experience of God at work within a believer's life.

Skeptics Answered D. James Kennedy
Dr. James Kennedy takes on some of the most-asked questions regarding the validity of the Christian faith and provides factual, well-reasoned answers.

Pursuit Magazine
A contemporary magazine for the seeker that offers a clear presentation of the gospel. Can be used as a tool for evangelism in community outreach campaigns.

Basic Christianity John Stott
Examine the historical facts on which Christianity stands.

Beyond Imagination: A Simple Plan to Save the World Dick Eastman
Documents amazing ways in which God is working throughout the world.

Bridge to Life
This booklet explains in easy-to-understand language that God loves all people but that sin separates us from Him and that the only way to God is through Jesus.

First Order of Business
Raise interest in the gospel at the workplace with this booklet featuring Scripture selections and faith stories of Christian business leaders.

How To Give Away Your Faith Paul Little
Motivates, instructs, and leads believers in this generation to share their living faith.

Life-Saving Card
A card you can distribute to believers who will pledge their desire and commitment to pray for non-Christians and share Jesus.

How to be a Successful Soul Winner C.S. Lovett
The letters "SOS" have been used for 16 decades to rescue people from physical peril–now SOS has a spiritual use, the Saving of Souls never to die again.

The Hole In America's Heart, I'll Be Home For Christmas, Making More of a Difference With The Rest of Your Life Ron Hutchcraft
Various timely messages on the relevance of the gospel to everyday living. A clear presentation of the gospel.

Inside the Mind of Unchurched Harry & Mary Lee Strobel
How to reach friends and family who avoid God and the church. Written by a former atheist.

Have You Considered Him, Can I Believe Christianity, What is Christianity, Christianity for the Open-Minded, Becoming a Christian, Why I Believe in Christ
Various Authors
Simple, honest explorations of the claims of Christ and other issues relating to Christian faith.

Introducing Jesus Peter Scazzero
This handbook includes all you need to start a Bible study group for people who want to know more about Christ.

Share Jesus Without Fear Willaim Fay & Ralph Hodge
Presents a natural, nonthreatening way to share the gospel that eliminates the pressure, the argument, and the fear of failure.

The Master Plan of Evengelism Robert Coleman
Principles of the great commission in the apostolic church of the book of Acts.

Operation Good Neighbor Rev. Dan Southern
Cassettes and tracts for personal witnessing.

NIV Paperback Bible
This complete NIV Bible is excellent for giveaways. Available in five cover designs.

Proclamation

Bridgebuilder: Evangelism & Counselor Training Course Handbook
Serve as counselors at evangelistic events and reach the lost through friendship evangelism.

Men's Easter Breakfast: "Arise with the Guys"
A ministry strategy that makes it easy for the men in your church/ministry/community to reach men for Christ in a nonthreatening way.

Challenge 2000 Youth Events
A series of youth stadium celebrations connecting youth across the country.

Christmas Gatherings Joyce Bademan
Evangelistic get-togethers for couples, women, or teens that are a natural way of sharing the love of Jesus Christ with neighbors, friends, coworkers, etc.

Crusade Evangelism & The Local Church Sterling Huston
This book identifies evangelism principles used by Billy Graham Crusades which apply to your local church or ministry.

Going Forward with Jesus Christ
New believers will take confident steps towards growth.

More Than a Carpenter Josh McDowell
A book for people who are skeptical about Jesus' deity, His resurrection, His claims on their lives. A great resource to share with seekers at proclamation events.

Y 2000
Discover why what happened 2000 years ago shapes history as we know it today. The story of Jesus in the powerful New Living Translation.

Celebrate Jesus 2000 New Testament (NLT)
The warmth of the Living Bible meets the accuracy of the King James Version. Ideal for new believers of all ages.

Preservation

TRAINING

Beginning Your Christian Life
A personal Bible study for new Christians, based on four lessons from John's Gospel.

The Friendship Principle
Designed to help the members of your church think through and discuss both personal and corporate friendliness to attract new believers.

Communicating Christ Effectively: Evangelism Training Manual
A tool for preparing churches to receive and disciple new believers following a saturation outreach for Easter 1999.

Nurturing New Believers
Like any good parent, God sends His babies to places that have a good "nursery." If we want to see rebirths in our church, we will need to be committed to "newborn care" of Christians.

The Master Plan of Discipleship
Traces basic principles of Jesus' strategy to reach the world through making disciples.

Preparing Your Church for New Christians
This booklet will help your church prepare to care for new followers of Jesus Christ.

Discipleship

Thirty Discipleship Excercises
A 30-lesson study featuring 30 different topics with six verses for each lesson on the same topic.

Beginning with Christ
A booklet of encouragement and assurances for the new Christian. Five important verses of assurance are presented for memorization along with a brief explanation of what the decision to accept Christ really means and the importance of God's Word.

Being A Christian, Christ In You, Encouraging New Christians Various Authors
Booklets to encourage new Christians in their faith-walk.

Going On with Christ
Introducing the young Christian to eight verses for memorization of important truths about our relationshop with Christ and those around us and what we need to do to serve and honor God.

Growing Strong in God's Family
The introductory course to the 2:7 Series. Designed for group study and leads new Christians through the basics of Christianity.

Interactions Bill Hybels
Small group series covering the fruit of the spirit, transformation, psalms, character, Jesus, and evangelism.

Knowing God J.I. Packer
This classic reveals the wonder, the glory, and the joy of knowing God.

Personal Follow-Up Set
Worksheet set containing five basic Christian principles for the new believer plus a leader's guide.

Stretching and Growing Charles R. Schumate
A thoughtful, biblical, and relational guide for the "new person in Christ" to think in a systematic manner about the meaning of his or her new commitment.

More Resources

The Ragamuffin Gospel Brennan Manning
Even as ragamuffins, the Father beckons us to Him with a "furious love" that burns brightly for His children. It is a gift like no other. It is only when we truly realize God's grace that we can forever bask in the unbridled joy of a gospel that enfolds the most needy of His ragamuffins.

Experiencing Spiritual Breakthroughs Bruce Wilkinson
In the midst of a society without morals, a passionate relationship with Jesus is possible—not just a "mountaintop experience," but an everyday vibrant relationship.

A Godward Life John Piper
A Godward Life is a passionate, moving, and articulate call for all believers to live their lives in conscious and glad submission to the sovereignty and glory of God.

Tender Commandments Ron Mehl
The Ten Commandments are often portrayed as ominous warnings—cold, harsh words from an all-powerful and vengeful God. This book recasts them as messages of love—ten declarations of our Creator's love for us.

Dawn 2000–7 Million Churches To Go James Montgomery
The personal story of the DAWN strategy to plant a church within easy access of every 400–1,000 people on earth by the end of the century.

Growing in Community
A discipleship-based line of Bible studies designed specifically to help a group become a small closely knit community motivated and empowered to worship and serve God.

Living Proof Discipleship (Video Series)
Takes you inside a small group that is intent on following Jesus and growing as His disciple. What it means to He His disciple in our contemporary culture.

Now That You Are His David Shibley
You have made a commitment of your life to Christ as Lord and Savior. "Now That You Are His," what specific things can you do to grow as a Christian? This book helps people take those important steps.

The Discipleship Series J. Reapsome
This Bible study series deals with the Christian disciplines that are vital to both new and mature Christians.

The First Year of Your Christian Life Steve Pogue
The first year of the Christian life is often the most difficult. In this book the author helps new believers sort through questions and problems and lays a foundation for a lifetime of walking with Christ.

The Purpose Driven Church Rick Warren
Books, tapes and curriculum for local churches to use in setting up their assimilation process.

Men & Women resources

Men's Ministry Manual
This manual has information on *Reach 3*, seminars, retreats, small group materials, training institutes, strategic planning calendars, discipleship, mentoring, and speakers.

Men's Ministry Action Plan
A leader's guide to help you create, capture, and sustain momentum in your church's men's ministry. Walks you through a process that will help you reach and disciple the men of your church more effectively.

Evengelism Syllabus Promise Keepers
To equip and empower men to understand and share the gospel with other men, and to assist in any evangelistic ministry in or around the local church.

Tender Warrior Stu Weber
Stu Weber paints a dramatic and compelling picture of balanced manhood according to God's blueprint.

Point Man Steve Farrar
If your family is going to make it through intact, they will need a trained, God-appointed leader at the point. So equip yourself for the battle. And learn how to lead your family successfully through the hazards and ambushes the enemy has planned.

What God Does When Men Pray Promise Keepers
A Promise Keepers guide that will challenge and awaken men within your men's ministry. It will not only challenge them to pray daily but it will also show them how this time of prayer will change their lives forever.

Moving Beyond Belief Various Authors
This resource is a 16-chapter workbook dealing with a man and his relationship to God as well as his relationship with himself, his relationship with others, and his relationship to the body of Christ.

The Fight John White
The Fight is an engaging Christian growth and discipleship book that will get new Christians started and draw more mature Christians deeper.

PK Men's NIV Study Bible
Start enjoying new benefits of personal, in-depth Bible study. Follow Scripture links and notes written by experienced Bible teachers.

Beginning Your Journey of Joy Bill & Vonnette Bright
A '90s version of the Four Spiritual Laws intended for women. Speaks the language of today's women and offers a slightly feminine approach to sharing God's love with neighbors, friends, and family members.

New Testament for Women
Introduce women to Christ with this elegant, single-column NIV New Testament with special helps written especially for women. Themed plan focusing on the heart issues of women.

Youth resources

Challenge 2000 Campus Starter Kit
Information and resources for beginning ministries to and with the young people in your community.

How to Get Better Grades and Have More Fun Steve Douglass
This book does much more than just tell young people how to get better grades. It shares that in times of anxiety and tough circumstances students can run to God for guidance and peace of mind every day.

Generating Hope
A strategy for reaching the postmodern generation. Explores the power of community, shame, adoption, and hope for young adults.

Jesus for a New Generation Kevin Graham Ford
Putting the gospel in the language of the Xers.

Pole 2 Locker Reach Out Ministries
Teach students to communicate their faith before the opportunity fades away.

The Battle For a Generation Ron Hutchcraft with Lisa Hutchcraft Whitmer
Provides knowledge, practical methods and a vision for reaching today's generation for Christ. This book gives an up-close look at the world of today's teenager.

The Answer
A simple, powerful presentation of the gospel. Millions have been shared around the world to lead people to *The Answer.*

Your Most Important Relationship
Booklet for evangelism. Available in English or Spanish.

How to Know God Personally
This tract is specifically desiged to help share God's great news about His desire for a relationship with us.

More Resources

Real Magazine
Having difficulties finding out who you are, what you want to do, where you want to go, how to love, where to give, and how to grow?

Sports Outreach resources

Motor Racing Resources
Olympic Resources
World Cup Resources
Women's World Cup Resources
Here is a wide range of ministry materials with a sports focus to use in evangelistic outreach.

Mickey Mantle: His Final Inning, CyberTract (ATS)
This CD-ROM shares his personal story.

Proclamation of Athletes
Link to your favorite Christian athlete's Web site to learn more about them and their personal faith.

Sports Spectrum Magazine RBC Ministries
Features top Christian athletes in a full-color magazine. Character-building content makes it perfect for fans of all ages.

Super Bowl Outreach Kit AIA, FCA, IBS, and Sports Spectrum
Ministry materials for churches and individuals to use in evangelistic outreach during the Super Bowl event. Kit items include a video, ten *More Than Winning* booklets, ten *Sports Spectrum* magazines, a poster for advertising your activity, and a planning guide.

Golf Videos
A series of 30-minute videos featuring professional golfers who give instructional golfing tips and share their personal testimony.

StraightTrax cassettes
Featured athletes—Reggie White, David Robinson, Michelle Akers, and others—share their personal testimony on an audiocassette. Great tool for ministering to youth.

One Way to Play
Faced daily with peer pressure and personal temptation, teenagers are often unsure of where to turn for help. "One Way to Play" offers them relief from the pressure, and encouragement to be responsible.

Path to Victory NIV New Testaments
These sports themed New Testaments include faith stories and favorite verses of world-famous Christian athletes, a 28-day reading plan, and a gospel presentation.

resources

City Profile
A profile to help cities determine where God is at work in their city.

Power of Partnership Phill Butler
Strategic evangelism and church planting partnerships hold the brightest hope for reaching the more than 2 billion people worldwide who have not had the opportunity to respond to Christ.

City Discovery Guide
A guide to help Christian leaders as together they seek the face and will of God for their city.

Mapping Center for Evangelism
Along with regional forms and training on computer mapping and outreach strategies, each member receives a variety of tools on CD-ROM to help you map both your mission field and mission force.

Real Hope in Chicago Wayne L. Gordon with Randall Frame
The incredible story of how the gospel is transforming a Chicago neighborhood. It offers an exciting model for interracial cooperation and urban-suburban church partnering.

Beyond Charity John M. Perkins
Not everyone is called to move to the inner city to minister there, but everyone is called to have a heart for its hurting people. This book shows people how to be sensitive to our brothers and sisters, and to come up with effective ministries.

That None Should Perish Ed Silvoso
A practical and biblical overview of prayer evangelism strategy as first experienced in Argentina and thoughtfully presented as a way to reach cities and nations all over the world.

A Theology as Big as the City Ray Bakke
What does Scripture have to say about urban ministry? Here is a biblical theology that will constantly surprise and challenge as you get a glimpse of how big God's view of the city really is.

The House of the Lord Francis Frangipane
This challenging book shows churches how to lay aside individual differences and doctrines and come together united in worship and warfare—to rebuild the house of the Lord and to bring healing.

Primary Purpose Ted Haggard
It's time to reach out to our communities and cities with the love and grace of Jesus Christ. Filled with inspiration and insights.

More Resources

God So Loves the City Charles Van Engen & Judy Tuiersma, Editors
The editors worked closely with an international team of urban practitioners to explore the most urgent issues facing those who minister in today's cities.

Loving Your City Into the Kingdom Ted Haggard and Jack Hayford
City-reaching strategies for a 21st century revival.

Restoring At-Risk Communities John M. Perkins
If you are already in the trenches of rebuilding a community, or if you are sensing God's call to such a ministry, this manual will serve as a compass and a source of encouragement.

The Urban Christian Ray Bakke with Jim Hart
This book offers the basic building blocks needed to love this young, rootless, mobile, media–turned population. Here is practical, time–tested wisdom on what the church can and is doing in worship, work, and witness.

Children resources

Celebrate the Child
A national evangelical campaign to heighten the awareness of the importance Jesus places on children.

Becoming a Child of God Pioneer Clubs
Pamphlet that explains John 3:16. (grades 1-6)

Bright Beginnings New Testament
Light up a child's life with this NIV New Testament. Features include computer-designed illustrations and an evangelism plan for kids. Great for Sunday School or VBS.

Bringing My World to Christ Commitment Folder Evangelical Covenant Church
Serves as a pledge to pray for and share with people who don't know Christ. A tear-off panel may be used as a dedication sheet.

Learning More About Jesus Pioneer Clubs
How to walk with Christ. (grades 3-6)

My Heart—Christ's Home Robert Munger with Carolyn Nystrom
This is Peter's amazing story of a week spent with Jesus. Now children can read and understand how Jesus becomes Lord over all of life.

Sharing God's Special Plan with Children
North American Mission Board.

Who Cares? Assemblies of God
A reproducible live-action outreach video for kids.

My Good News Journal
A journal for children who are new Christians.

Now That I'm a Christian Cos Davis, William Young
Leader's guide. Provides a plan to guide children in grades 1-6 toward a genuine, growing Christian faith.

Scripture Union
Quest: Daily Bible readings for 7-10 year olds. One to One: Relevant daily readings for 1-14 year olds. AM-PM: Visual daily readings for 14-18 year olds.

More Resources

Belonging to God's Family
How to grow as a Christian. (grades 1-2)

The Born Again Birthday Book
Creative Children's Ministries

Music & Video resources

Celebrate Jesus 2000 Music Collection
Music products revolving around the evangelistic theme of Celebrate Jesus 2000. Includes cassettes and

CDs for listening, accompaniment, and promotion. Also available are a choral book and orchestration.

Repeat Performance

A great movie to teach young people about forgiving and being forgiven. A suspense-filled ride with a young man whose life has gone from bad to worse. He's the main suspect in a fatal hit and run. Only the incredible forgiveness of God can save him now.

The Home Coming

A humorous yet touching look at peer pressure. Jordy Rembrandt is a big-city tough guy with an attitude and a history of bad decisions. When he's sent to a small-town high school to finish his senior year, Jordy discovers "fitting in" takes on a new meaning.

Cry from the Mountain

Great wilderness adventure that brings a family together under God. An exciting father-son kayak trip in the Alaskan wild turns into a dramatic test of faith in the white-water rapids.

Scars that Heal: The Dave Roever Story

An amazing story of spiritual and physical healing following Roever's devastating accident in Vietnam. Only the love of God and his wife gave him hope.

God's Story: From Creation to Eternity

A breathtaking journey through the Bible. Dramatic visuals combined with live action, special effects, and original music score. This evangelistic film bridges all age groups and cultures.

The Search, I Gotta Tell You Something Kevin Can Wait

These titles and other evangelistic videos, books, and computer software available.

Ethnic & Reconciliation resources

Healing America's Wounds John Dawson

This book shows how the open wounds of our past and present are bleeding the life from America. Discover how you can play a part in breaking the chain of sin handed down for generations.

An American Friend Handbook

This publication will answer many questions and give an overview of what is involved in befriending an international student—from making the first contact to sharing the gospel, and virtually everything in between.

Becoming a Friend with an International Student

This booklet will help you see how your friendship can make a world of difference in the life of a student, in your own life, and for eternity's sake.

Reconciliation Resources Catalog C. DeYoung

This catalog of books, videos, and audiotapes encourages ministry in urban and multicultural settings.

More Than Equals Spencer Perkins & Chris Rice

Racial healing for the sake of the gospel.

One New People Manuel Oritz

Models for developing a multiethnic church.

How to Survive in the U.S.

A welcome kit for international students. It contains $20–30 of materials to give students multiple pathways to the gospel. Last year's kit included: New Testament, *JESUS* video soundtrack, *How to Survive in the U.S.*

booklet, How to Get Better Grades cassette, testimonial video, coupons, and giveaways.

More Resources

Reaching Students from the People's Republic of China
This booklet is designed to help you understand some basics about your Chinese friend. It will help you to be a sensitive and effective witness for Jesus Christ.

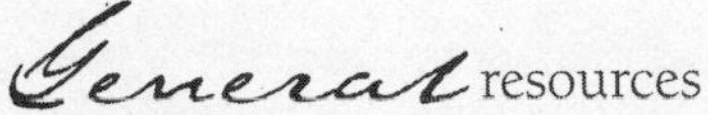

resources

1999: Year of The Bible
An exciting plan to encourage people to spend five minutes a day to read the entire New Testament in 1999.

A Revival Primer Dale Schlafer
It will stimulate your interest in revival so that you might be motivated to read further and understand more about this subject that affects you and your church.

Rivers of Revival Neil A. Anderson & Elmer L. Towns
Answers what many Christians are asking today, "What will it take to see revival?" Examines the fascinating subject of personal revival, and past and current evangelistic streams that could help usher in global revival.

The Coming Revival Bill Bright
Fasting and praying by millions of God's people can usher in a mighty, spiritual revival and awakening and lift His judgement from upon our land.

Total Church Life Darrell Robinson
How to be a first-century church in a 21st-century world. A crucial guide to knowing and nurturing the 12 vital signs of a healthy church.

Stand in the Gap, How to Prepare for the Coming World Revival David Bryant
More than just a call for revival or a yearning for revival. It is a curriculum and preparatory guide for revival.

March for Jesus
March for Jesus is a worldwide worship celebration for Jesus Christ. It is a joyous celebration of our Lord Jesus Christ with prayer for our cities and nations.

Access to God
This booklet, with an introduction from Joni Eareckson Tada, will help you share Christ with the disabled.

More Resources

Messengers of Hope, Becoming Agents of Revival for the 21st Century David Bryant
Through his worldwide Concerts of Prayer, David Bryant has seen impossible situations transformed by a spiritual awakening. Now he's equipping all denominations and ethnic groups to become messengers of hope.

Once in a Lifetime David Shirley
This book is a passionate twenty–first century trumpet call for the church to finally fulfill the great commission—in our lifetime! This challenge contains cutting–edge insight into how you can help make it happen.

Thank You

for being a part of
The Lighthouse Movement—
an unprecedented movement of God!

Two ways to join:

- Register on the Internet at
www.lighthousemovement.com

- Or complete the attached form and
return it in an envelope to the following address:

THE LIGHTHOUSE MOVEMENT
5666 LINCOLN DRIVE SUITE 100
EDINA MN 55436

The Lighthouse Movement Registration Card

Yes, I will be a Lighthouse and help reach the goal of sharing Jesus with every person in America by year-end 2000! Please register me:

Name ______________________________

Address ______________________________

City ______________________________

State ________________ Zip Code __________

Phone (______)____________ E-mail __________

Welcome to the Lighthouse Movement! Your commitment to pray, care, and share is all that is needed to be a Lighthouse. To register your Lighthouse and for free downloadable Lighthouse information, go to the official Lighthouse website at www.lighthousemovement.com. Use this form to order you Lighthouse Resource Kit for a gift of $10. To help recruit at least three million Lighthouses, please consider making an additional gift. *Thank you!*

☐ I'm sending a gift to help expand The Lighthouse Movement. I'm enclosing:
☐$15 ☐$25 ☐$75
☐Other$_____

☐ I'm enclosing $10 to order The Lighthouse Resource Kit containing a prayer journal, lapel pin, bumper sticker, calendar with helpful tips, and subscription to *The Lighthouse Newsletter*.

Total amount enclosed: $__________
(Make checks payable to Mission America)

☐ I prefer to use my credit card.
Please bill the total to my:
☐VISA ☐MasterCard ☐AMEX
☐Discover

Card Number ____________________ Exp. Date _____

Signature ______________________________

☐ I want to help recruit more Lighthouses.
Please send me ______ Lighthouse brochures.

☐ Please contact me about being the Lighthouse representative for my church. *(over)*

The Lighthouse Movement Registration Card

Yes, I will be a Lighthouse and help reach the goal of sharing Jesus with every person in America by year-end 2000! Please register me:

Name ______________________________

Address ______________________________

City ______________________________

State ________________ Zip Code __________

Phone (______)____________ E-mail __________

Welcome to the Lighthouse Movement! Your commitment to pray, care, and share is all that is needed to be a Lighthouse. To register your Lighthouse and for free downloadable Lighthouse information, go to the official Lighthouse website at www.lighthousemovement.com. Use this form to order you Lighthouse Resource Kit for a gift of $10. To help recruit at least three million Lighthouses, please consider making an additional gift. *Thank you!*

☐ I'm sending a gift to help expand The Lighthouse Movement. I'm enclosing:
☐$15 ☐$25 ☐$75
☐Other$

☐ I'm enclosing $10 to order The Lighthouse Resource Kit containing a prayer journal, lapel pin, bumper sticker, calendar with helpful tips, and subscription to *The Lighthouse Newsletter*.

Total amount enclosed: $__________
(Make checks payable to Mission America)

☐ I prefer to use my credit card.
Please bill the total to my:
☐VISA ☐MasterCard ☐AMEX
☐Discover

Card Number ____________________ Exp. Date _____

Signature ______________________________

☐ I want to help recruit more Lighthouses.
Please send me ______ Lighthouse brochures.

☐ Please contact me about being the Lighthouse representative for my church. *(over)*

If you will please share the following information with Mission America, we will keep it confidential:

The following information will help us track involvement in The Lighthouse Movement. All information is confidential:

Please tell us the name, address and denomination of the church you attend:

Church Name______________________________

Address__________________________________

City_______________ State___ Zip code_______

Denomination:____________________________

Pastor's name:____________________________

How did you hear about The Lighthouse Movement?

____

____

____

____

____

____

Any additional comments _________________

____

____

____

____

The Lighthouse Movement subscribes to the DMA Association's Guidelines for Personal Information Protection. You will receive a receipt for your tax deductible contribution.

If you will please share the following information with Mission America, we will keep it confidential:

The following information will help us track involvement in The Lighthouse Movement. All information is confidential:

Please tell us the name, address and denomination of the church you attend:

Church Name______________________________

Address__________________________________

City_______________ State___ Zip code_______

Denomination:____________________________

Pastor's name:____________________________

How did you hear about The Lighthouse Movement?

____

____

____

____

____

____

Any additional comments _________________

____

____

____

____

The Lighthouse Movement subscribes to the DMA Association's Guidelines for Personal Information Protection. You will receive a receipt for your tax deductible contribution.